A PILGRIM PEOPLE

A PILGRIM PEOPLE

Learning Through the Church Year

John H. Westerhoff, III

THE SEABURY PRESS

Library of Congress Catalog Card Number: 84-51081

ISBN: 0-86683-884-8

Printed in the United States of America

5 4 3 2 1

The Seabury Press
430 Oak Grove
Minneapolis, Minnesota 55403

To the
parishioners, priests, and deacons of
the Chapel of the Cross,
Chapel Hill, North Carolina;
the students, faculty, and staff of
the Duke University Divinity School,
Durham, North Carolina,
with whom I have celebrated God's story
and shared life's stories
on a common journey in faith;
and the friends
with whom I first shared these reflections
in 1982 at Kanuga,
an Episcopal conference center
in Hendersonville, North Carolina

Contents

One

God's Story as Our Story

Richard Adams' novel *Watership Down*, ostensibly an adventure story about rabbits, is really about the conditions necessary for a viable community, namely, the ability to sustain the narrative that defines its life. *Watership Down* begins with an exodus, a hazardous journey in search of a new home, ultimately, Watership Down. The rabbits move out as a group of separate individuals, each with its own reasons for leaving. They become a people, a community, as they acquire a story. And they remain a community so long as they retell their story.

So it is with us. Our identity is dependent on having a story that tells us who we are; our understanding of life's meaning and purpose is dependent on having a story that tells us what the world is like and where we are going. To be a community of faith, we must be a people with a story: a common memory and vision, common rituals or symbolic actions expressive of our community's memory and vision, and a common life together that manifests our community's memory and vision.

The church is a story-formed community. Baptism is our adoption into a story, God's recreative story, which is recorded in the community's story book (the Holy Scriptures), incarnate in the community's life, and made present through its sacramental rituals, especially the Holy Eucharist. Each of us also has a story. To each community Eucharist we bring our stories and reenact God's story so that God's story and our stories may be made one story. In the context of our liturgies we are initiated into God's story and we appropriate its significance for our lives so that it might influence our common life day by day. And as we journey through history and traverse life-cycle passages, the retelling of God's story sustains us and moves us on.

Our most important and fundamental task as Christians is to learn God's story. All our Christian beliefs, experiences, and action are dependent upon our internalization of God's story, that is, making God's story our story. This explains why for a number of years I have described the first aim of catechesis as the acquisition and appropriation of God's recreative story, through participation in the church's rituals and through reflection on the intersection of our life stories and God's story, so that we individually and corporately may more faithfully manifest God's story in our lives.

All of this may seem obvious, but it has not been normative in the church's life and learning. I am continually surprised at how few people in the church know God's story or are able to express how their stories and God's story touch and inform each other. More important perhaps, I have discovered that even those who claim interest in God's story as found in the church's story book, the Holy Scriptures, are more interested in doctrine than sacred story. The temptation of theology is to interpret the foundational stories of the Christian faith and then treat the interpretations as if they were that which was originally given. Theology is founded on thoughts and concepts that, if taken overseriously, will replace the stories that make faith and community possible and will replace them with dogma and institutions. Indeed, the vast majority of books on the church year turn out to be books primarily on doctrine, as do the majority of so-called "Bible-centered" curriculum resources.

Did you ever try to discuss the Bible with a literalist? For literalists there is no story, no poetry, no imagination, only doctrinal truths to be believed, that is, to be asserted intellectually as true. The Bible for them becomes a collection of proof texts for doctrine, ideas about God to be believed rather than a story book to be dramatized and lived out within a story-formed community. Indeed, to say that the

Bible is essentially myth or sacred story *(true story)*—that is, history but much more—is offensive to many. Sacred story, or God's story as found in the Holy Scriptures, embraces history but is not merely history. Sacred stories are destroyed when taken literally, for their function is to point beyond themselves to God and to bring the experience of God into our present.

The stories were not collected by the church as a theology textbook. Nothing can replace a story. Stories resist definitive interpretation and invite commentary. Theology is abstract but not story; story invites participation. We discuss theology but experience story. Theological speculation limits and divides; story frees and unites. Only adults can engage in meaningful theological reflection. Stories are for all ages. "Tell me a story" is the request of every child. At the heart of the Christian faith is story, not dogma.

The major roles in Peter Shaffer's play *Equus* are an adolescent boy and his psychiatrist. The young man has blinded a number of horses after being seduced by a woman employee of the stable. The psychiatrist's task is to analyze the cause of this psychotic behavior and free the young man for productive life. What is unveiled in the drama is the mental torment of a patient and the story he developed to make it tolerable. The psychiatrist comments, "We need a story to see in the dark." We all need such a story. Stories are the means by which we see reality. Without a story it would appear as if we lived in an unreal world. Without a story we cannot live. Without a story we cannot have community. In the beginning is a story that provides us with both a memory linking us meaningfully with the past and a vision calling us to a purposeful future. Without a story life makes no sense. The story that is foundational to our life provides us with the basis for our perceptions and for our faith. Faith is manifested in story; story communicates faith. Anyone familiar with Chaucer's *Canterbury Tales* will remember that the pilgrims told stories on the way to the shrine of St. Thomas à Becket. Stories are the imaginative way of ordering our experience. The pilgrimage of life requires a story.

The Gospel began as a narrative including stories, sayings, songs, and interpretations remembered by those who had experienced life with Jesus of Nazareth and had concluded that he was the Christ. Later these were collected and arranged for various purposes (Matthew as a catechism for Jewish Christians and Luke as a catechism for Gentile Christians, Mark as a spiritual journal, and John as a witness to sacrament) written down, and in the end authorized for inclusion in the church's canon. Christianity is based upon and arises out of that story; the church's faith and life are first communicated by and later conceptualized through its story. Still it remains a story handed down from generation to generation as a symbolic narrative that forms and transforms our perceptions, evokes images, frees our imaginations, and thereby turns daily life into holy history.

Stories are concrete and particular. They are not expressions of doctrine or universal truth. Stories are open-ended. They are not to be read literally; as a matter of fact, stories give the storyteller freedom in their retelling. Stories stimulate the imagination. There is not only one interpretation of a story; indeed, the listener is encouraged to listen freely and discover personal meaning. Stories are experiential. They are told by a participant, and they are to be participated in. Stories are the bottom line of human communal life: Nothing else is ultimately needed.

The Bible is a storybook. Basically, it is a love story between God and humanity; it is a story of a covenant made, broken, and renewed, again and again. God as creator, redeemer, and perfecter loves each creature, personally and as members of the whole human community. In return, we are expected to love God ourself, and each other.

The Bible is a book of faith; that is, the Bible presents a way to perceive life in general and our lives in particular. The Bible is a book of revelation; that is, the Bible unveils those intimate relationships with God experienced by others so that we might share in them. The Bible is a book of vocation; that is, the Bible gives us a vision of how we ought to live our lives with God and each other day by day.

We need to enlarge our grasp of this love story—to learn it more completely, to understand it more deeply, to possess it more personally, and to live it more fully. This is a lifelong task. But the place to begin is always the same: We need to learn to tell the story as our story. And the purpose of our learning to do so is always the same: to transform individual and social life so that God's will might be done and God's reign might come.

As a storybook, the Bible is made up of various kinds of stories. They are myths, apologies, narratives, and parables, to name four. Each serves a different and unique function.

The function of myth is to establish our world. Myths explain that this is the way life really is, in spite of any evidence to the contrary. Myths are not false stories. In fact, as the Pawnee Indians were wise to point out, it is history that is composed of false stories; myths are true stories, because they are about God; they are more than history in that they point beyond history to its meaning. The stories of Jesus' birth and resurrection are myths. They explain the meaning and purpose of life. They are true stories, in the most important sense of those words, for they explain our world. Everyone lives by some collection of myths. No one finds meaning or purpose in life without them.

Apologetic stories defend our myths. They are primarily biographical, for what better defense is there for a particular way of envisioning life than the lives of those who believe it and live by it? It is difficult to argue with the person who is willing to suffer and die for a particular way of understanding life and its meaning. That is why the stories of the saints, the ancient and modern heroes of the faith, are also important to know and share.

Narrative stories explore the world that our myths establish and the biographies of believers defend. For example, one myth may tell us that God is a merciful and loving God, but our experience may indicate otherwise. Narratives explore these contradictions and in the end reaffirm the myth. The story of Job is a perfect example.

And last, there are parables whose function is to subvert the way our culture sees life so that we might perceive the world in ways consistent with our myths. For example, the second half of the Jonah story and Jesus' story of the vineyard have a similar message: God does not give us what we deserve, but what we need. That is consistent with the Judeo-Christian myth of a gracious and merciful God, but it is subversive to those of us who live in a reward-and-punishment world. This world defines justice as getting what you deserve and has difficulty supporting welfare for fear people will get something they do not deserve.

Of course, there are other sorts of material in the Bible, such as prophetic judgments on persons and communities who live lives that violate the implications of the community's myths. There are songs and prayers that celebrate life as it is lived within the context of our myths, and there are words of wisdom gleaned from experience that support the community's myth. But at the heart of it all is a love story, the Christian myth that must be known, owned, and lived if we are to be Christian.

Our greatest human need and most difficult achievement is to find meaning in our lives. An understanding of the meaning of life is not suddenly acquired at a particular age. At every point in our lives, we need to discover some meaning. The whole process begins in childhood, when we learn through stories. To hold our attention, a story must entertain us and arouse our curiosity, but to enrich our lives, it must stimulate our imaginations and provide us with ever new and deeper meanings. Stories emerge from and speak to our responsive, intuitive consciousness. That is why it is meaningless to take our sacred stories or our symbolic narratives literally; it is equally meaningless to try intellectually to discover their meaning by searching for what can be rationally verified in them. Sacred stories speak to our deepest, unconscious longings and questions, our problems and predicaments, our inner and outer struggles in human life. They exist in the form of truth that only intuition and imagination can provide, truth just as significant and real as the truth that comes through logical analysis and scientific probing.

The Bible story is a symbolic narrative. That is why it enlightens us about ourselves and fosters our growth. It offers meaning on varying levels and enriches our lives in countless ways. The meanings of each story will change at different times in our lives; insights will vary, depending on our needs and experiences at the moment. That is why it is a mistake to explain a story or tack on a moral at its close. When we use the Bible to indoctrinate people, we destroy the story and do injustice to the Scriptures. When we simply tell stories without explanations, people want to hear the stories over and over again. And when we have derived all we can from a story, we will temporarily set it aside until it becomes relevant once again.

It is important for us to remember that both children and adults need stories. It is human nature to order our lives in accordance with a story. Stories make sense out of the chaos of life on the level of the unconscious; that is, poetic stories provide our imaginations with the means of ordering our experiences. They leave us open to new insights and inspirations. Stories preserve the memory of past events and the experiences to help shape our lives.

Stories are fundamentally oral and communal in nature. They are meant to be told, dramatized, sung, danced, and expressed through the visual arts. They are not intended only to be read. We forget that the biblical story was written down only because the community was worried that its storytellers would forget the story, distort the story, or neglect some important aspects of it. We need to return to telling and celebrating our story as a people of God.

Stories are of central importance in human life, and they are enacted through our rituals. We humans cannot live without ritual; our religious life is expressed collectively through symbolic narratives (sacred stories) and symbolic actions (rituals and ceremonies). Perhaps no aspect of life is more important than our ceremonial life. We humans are made for ritual, and our rituals make us. No community exists without a shared story and shared repetitive symbolic actions. Our understandings and our ways are invariably objectified in ceremonial observances. Faith and ritual cannot be separated. Thus, when the prophets sensed that the people were forsaking their faith, they attacked the rituals as empty substitutes. But when the people had lost their faith, the prophets called them to return to their rituals. Without rituals, we lack a means for building and establishing purposeful identity; we are devoid of any significant way to sustain and transmit our understandings. Rituals, like stories, emerge from and speak to our intuitive, emotional consciousness. That explains why dance, drama, music, and visual arts are the basic means by which our rituals are enacted. And that is why poetry more than prose is the basic means by which ritual is expressed in words. When worship becomes too intellectual or wordy, it loses its depth and significance.

One of the problems in Western culture, especially post-reformation Enlightenment culture, is that it is ocular in nature; that is, it is a book-oriented culture that reads and writes. We speak of the "eyes of faith" and hold that "seeing is believing." We are wordy and our preaching is discursive. We turn sacred story into historical event and doctrinal statement. We produce persons who use the biblical story as pornography (a subject turned into an object) or as idolatry (a means turned into an end). In an oral culture, on the other hand, learning involves all the senses and the imagination as well. In an oral culture truth is poetic, and story-telling is understood as the doorway into the realm of the sacred. Persons in an oral culture experience life as whole, integrated and interconnected. The biblical story becomes a sacred story that is to be imagined and participated in, not studied objectively or believed literally. Oral cultures understand that rituals are symbolic actions, expressive of the community's story, that thereby preserve the memory of past events and the anticipation of future events in ways that have power to make sense out of life in the present. Ritual story-telling is every community's primal way of knowing.

We humans live in two worlds: the world of outward events or visible manifestations and the world of inner experience or spiritual reality. To be human is to integrate the inner world of imagination, intuition, and subjective experience with the outer world of interpretive, intellectual, objective reflection and moral action. Similarly, Scriptures are a record of events and a witness to religious experience in the form of a sacred narrative. It is the re-presentation of this symbolic narrative or sacrament that integrates the inner and outer worlds by producing an outward and visible manifestation of an inner spiritual reality.

The church is a story-formed community, a people on pilgrimage through time, through seasons of profane time made holy by the eternal cycle of sacred time. The manner in which we order and use time is the best indicator of what is important to us. Time both expresses and shapes our lives. We live in time. We find time for what we consider important, and how we spend our time influences our understandings and ways of life. We recall and celebrate the occasions that are most significant to us, and the days we celebrate give meaning and purpose to our lives.

There are, of course, those churches whose time is occupied with various promotional events, much like the calendar of a department store: Stewardship Sunday, Children's Day, Missionary Sunday, Evangelism Sunday, and the like. Institutional maintenance seems to be their primary concern. And there are those churches that celebrate only birthdays and forget baptism days, and make more of rally day, Mother's Day, Thanksgiving Day, and Independence Day than they do of the Transfiguration, Ascension Day, Holy Cross Day, the festival of the Holy Innocents, and various saints' days.

Nevertheless, it is the eternal cycle of the church year with its re-presentation of God's story in interaction with our human story that best orders our lives within a Christian faith community. One of the fundamental aims of liturgy is to help us to relive God's story in such a way that it touches, illumines, and transforms our human story and thereby shapes our lives to serve God's purposes for personal and communal life. And that is the aim of this small book, a rather simple attempt to comment on God's story, the good news as contained in the church's lectionary canon, relating it to our human stories as we travel together through the eternal cycle of sacred time as celebrated in the church year. It is at best the sharing of a personal pilgrimage through a year in the church's liturgical life with the hope that it will stimulate the imagination and touch the hearts and minds of other pilgrims who travel each year over the same route in search of meaning and purpose. In the last chapter, I will make a somewhat radical proposal for church life, worship, education (catechesis), and witness, but for now, the story.

Two

A New Beginning

When most people think of the beginning of the church's story, they think of Advent. We seem to forget that no matter how important the incarnation and Christmas, it was Easter that gave birth to our Christian faith. Without the story of Easter, the story of Christmas is meaningless. From the very beginning, Christian faith has rested on the mystery of Christ's passion, death, and resurrection. "Christ has died, Christ is risen, Christ will come again" is our Eucharistic acclamation. The church's story begins and ends with the Easter proclamation; indeed, no matter what other aspect of the story we are remembering, each Lord's Day Eucharist is an Easter celebration, a feast of the Paschal mystery.

Through the Easter story we remember the dream come true, the vision become reality, the fullness of life made present; we realize the intentions of creation fulfilled, the sovereign reign of God established. This Easter story is a story of a new creation, a world in which peace and justice, liberation and reconciliation, equity and unity, and the well-being of all people are established. The power of cosmic, social, and personal evil has been defeated. All humanity is made whole and holy, redeemed from captivity to sin, born anew, reestablished in the image of God, infused with the Spirit of God, made saints empowered to be signs and witnesses to a new world and a new humanity, adopted by God to witness to the truth about the world and each person in it. The Easter story is a story of the victory of God, a story that brings together the stories of God entering our human life and history, and of God's future consummation of all human life and history through the passion, death, and resurrection of Jesus Christ.

We enter the Week of Salvation, as the Orthodox call it, with a story of a cosmic drama, a royal passion (Mark 14:32-15:47). It is not a tragic tale but a majestic story of how Jesus' passion and death serves God's will and purpose. Jesus, the Christ of God, confronts the principalities and powers that distort God's reign, and through the mystery of his passion and death he fulfills the hopes of humanity for *shalom*. God acts in Jesus to deliver, redeem, and save the world and all its inhabitants from that which distorts human life and prevents God's will from being accomplished. It is a great drama about the victory of good over evil, light over darkness, wholeness over brokenness, freedom over oppression, community over estrangement, love over hate, life over death.

To tell the story honestly, we need to uproot every possible seed of anti-Semitism. It was not the Jews who killed Jesus. Indeed, in the mystery of Christ's passion and death, there is no need to establish a scapegoat; He, and He alone, is our scapegoat: the lamb of God who carries the sins of all humanity out of the world. We must never forget that Jesus was executed for political reasons by the political authorities. While he had no ambition to be an earthly king, the politicians were well aware how visionaries can disrupt the *status quo*. To bear the sign of God's liberating power is always to be a threat to those who benefit from life as it is.

To tell the story faithfully we need to remember that it is more a story about the evil we participate in than about some particular evil people long ago. Those who crucified Jesus were confronted by complex moral issues and decided on what they believed to be best for all under unfortunate circumstances. The most serious evil in this world is done by those who think they are doing good, or at least the best they can, in a less than perfect world. Jesus suffers because of our moral compromises.

The old story tells what happens today: leaders act to protect position and privilege; justice is corrupted; betrayal and cowardice are acted out; the victim is blamed and brutalized. It is a story that touches our story. We inflict pain on each other, we compromise wth injustice, we betray, we abandon, we accept the necessity of violence, we ignore suffering, we evade responsibility.

But if we pay attention only to these themes of the passion, we will miss the reason why the church remembers the passion story. The story of the passion ends in death, and so it is true to life. But the story has another dimension. It is also the story of how the passion of Jesus frees us to accept the broken reality of human life as the context in which God is forever making all things new. It is ultimately a story about how God enters our broken, distorted lives in order to transform them.

The passion story is a marvelous story of how we live in the mysterious paradox of acknowledging the most awful realities of life, never surprised by the awful condition of this world, yet remaining full of awe at the transforming power of sacrificial love. We cannot and ought not to evade the passion themes in our own lives and histories: the threat of nuclear holocaust, personal infidelity, the decline in a sense of public service, the loss of personal integrity, racism, sexism, nationalism—the list goes on. We are realists who retell the story; we know what human beings can do to ourselves and to one another. We are well aware that justice and peace can be trampled down. Evil in ourselves and in our world is strong indeed. Our human story knows no romantic optimism. No rope trick of positive thinking can escape the presence of evil in our midst.

Nevertheless we tell the story, because it is also a story about what God does in the midst of our brokenness. God takes that brokenness into God's self and thereby makes all things new. That is the story line that runs through the passion narrative. It is not easy to perceive that truth amidst the wreckage of our lives. That is why we keep retelling the story of how Christ died for us and thereby lives for us: that we might live the stories of our own lives with hope and courage. The story of the passion ends in death, but it is a story of a victory through death that frees us to accept the truth about ourselves and our world. So it is that there is good news in the passion; good news that if we can accept the brokenness in our lives and die a bit, we can be freed from it and grow again.

In the passion story we come to Holy Thursday (John 13:1-15). On this holy night we reenact the last meal of Jesus with his disciples and recall that he presented them with a farewell gift in his washing of their feet—a visible mandate to love in a manner that is as difficult to understand as it is to live.

The television production of the novel *The Thorn Birds* makes that difficulty clear. In commenting on the movie, Father Andrew Greeley makes the point that Father Ralph's worst sins are not of the flesh but of the spirit: ambition and insensitivity. *The Thorn Birds* is about a harsh, insensitive, ambitious priest who is saved by the humanization he experiences in the love of Maggie. The love is sinful, to be sure, though not nearly as sinful as his crass and cruel ambition. But the God who draws straight with crooked lines uses this illicit love affair to attract Ralph to his Creator. In the providence of a tricky, persistent, irresistibly loving God, Maggie—sinner or not—becomes for Ralph grace, sacrament, salvation. Thus *The Thorn Birds* is really about an implacably passionate God who will stop at nothing in the pursuit of creatures with whom God has fallen in love. And—says the story of this holy night in this holy week—we are to love in a similar manner.

Morton Kelsey, Episcopal priest, Jungian therapist, and spiritual theologian, tells of flying home from a conference in North Carolina. All at once he became aware that he was flying over the house of his brother from whom he was estranged, then over the home of his father and stepmother from whom he was also estranged, to see his teenage daughter on the advice of a friend who had counseled him to try to mend that relationship. Sitting in the quiet and mulling over this folly of spoiled relationships, the words of a prayer attributed to St. Francis rang in Kelsey's memory: "O divine Master, grant that I may not so much seek to be consoled as to console, to be understood as to understand, to be loved as to love." He comments that wave after wave of insight broke over him. He realized how much more interested he had been in receiving consolation and love than in giving them. If someone did not give him what he needed, he believed the relationship had failed. He realized, then, that emotional and spiritual maturity begin when we give love without expecting anything in return. Only when we forget status, reverse roles, and wash each other's feet; only when we forsake ambition, pride, and greed and give ourselves in acts of unselfish love can we experience life that is whole and holy. So it is that our stories and God's story once again intersect in our human pilgrimage, and each year on Holy Thursday we re-present the story to make real once again God's love for us and to illustrate how we should love.

It has been a grace in my life to pass through the Chapel of the Cross in Chapel Hill, North Carolina, where I am a priest associate, and find a host of folk who are not members of the congregation making the church their home. Here I have observed the thirsty drinking free coffee, the hungry taking their places in the line at a parish supper, the tired sleeping on a couch, the cold seeking warmth, the sick waiting for parents to pick them up, the homeless finding a home, if only for a night.

I've also observed that on occasion these folk inconvenience us, mess up our building, and frighten us. Nevertheless, I continue to pray that our parish may always be blessed by these wandering, sometimes staggering folk who pass through our open doors. I thank God for their sometimes disturbing presence, because they offer us the chance to share love and hospitality with those who have no status and can do nothing for us. I hope that we will never have so much pride in our building that we will worry about what these folk might inadvertently destroy. I hope we will never want so badly to prosper that we will seek to attract only people like ourselves and thereby make the outsiders feel ill at ease in our midst.

Each year as we retell God's story, we are reminded that we are called to be a community of love where washing feet is a way of life and not merely a yearly ritual act. Mother Teresa of Calcutta reminds us that when we give bread to the dying we love truly, for they can give us nothing in return. In holding them and feeding them we give them more than bread; we give them love. To be a Christian community is to be a people who strive to make sure there are no strangers or estranged among us. It is to create a space where each seeks to love rather than to be loved, and where the outcasts of the world can come to have their feet washed by those who have made it; only when we are such a community will we embody the story we tell and become story for the world.

From the story of Holy Thursday we proceed to the story of Good Friday, or Great Friday as it is called in the Eastern church (John 18:1-19:37). Listening to another story may help us to understand this story better. Toward the end of Helen Waddell's novel *Peter Abelard,* we find Peter and Theobald walking through the woods. A terrible cry, like the scream of a child in agony, attracts their attention. Peter finds a small rabbit caught in a trap. He sets the rabbit free, and as he does, the rabbit hops into his arms, nuzzles against his chest, and dies. Peter, with tears in his eyes says, "Theobald, do you think there is a God? Whatever has come to me, I deserve, but what did this one do?"

Theobald nods, "I know, only I think God is in it too."

Abelard looks up. "Do you mean that it makes God suffer the way it does us?"

Again Theobald nods. "All this," he strokes the limp body, "is because of us, but all the time God suffers more than we do."

Abelard looks at him, perplexed. "Theobald, do you mean Calvary?"

"Oh, that was only a piece of it, the piece we saw in time," says Theobald as he points over to a fallen tree sawn through the middle. "See the dark ring there? There it goes up and down the whole length of the tree but we only see it where it cuts across. That's what Christ's life was, a bit of God we saw. We think God is like that forever because it happened once with Christ. But not the pain, the agony: somehow we think that has stopped."

Abelard looks at him. "Then, Theobald, do you think all this suffering, all this pain of the world was Christ's cross—God's cross? O God, if only it were true" (Helen Waddell, *Peter Abelard,* New York: Holt and Co., 1933, p. 201 ff.).

The story of Good Friday brings us in touch with the story of suffering in our own lives and in those around us. And it tells us that we are not alone. God is with us dying, suffering, hurting, starving, weeping throughout the world. The presence and power of God is behind the suffering we know and in the suffering of Jesus. To suffer and die is Jesus' ministry to humanity. In the cross God is seen for who God is. In the death of Christ we find the greatest expression of God's love for us. Jesus' death on a cross, symbolic of his whole sacrificial life, is at the heart of our story.

At our baptism we were made Christians and branded with the sign of the crucified one to remind us that we have been baptized into Christ's suffering. The story of the crucifixion is at the heart of what it means to be a Christian. As the text of a new hymn reads:

Each newborn servant of the crucified
  bears on the brow the seal of him who died;
So shall our song of triumph ever be:
  praise to the crucified for victory.
So lift high the cross, the love of God proclaim
till all the world adores his sacred name.
                    (George W. Kitchin and Michael R. Newbolt)

Beginning at the Easter vigil and continuing throughout the great fifty days, the Paschal Candle, symbol of the risen Christ, stands prominent and lofty in the middle of the Eucharistic hall. But into that candle five nails will be driven to signify the wounds inflicted upon Jesus at his crucifixion. The story of Good Friday is never to be forgotten or ignored; indeed it is to be present always. The resurrection is not in spite of the crucifixion; it is because of it. The resurrection does not eliminate the crucifixion; it encompasses it. In the Christian story the wounds of Jesus never disappear. "Look at my hands and feet; it is really I," says Jesus. It may strike us as strange at first, but after the resurrection Jesus manifests himself as the crucified one. Jesus reveals his wounds as evidence of his pain and glory, his humiliation and exaltation. The point of Easter is that the crucified one lives, precisely *as* the crucified one.

It would be inappropriate to celebrate the Way of the Cross on Good Friday. As appropriate as it is to pray this ancient devotion each Friday during Lent, Great Friday is not oriented toward a sorrowful pilgrimage along the Via Dolorosa. Great Friday reminds us that Jesus does not need our sympathy. It would be arrogant to think that we can suffer for the one who suffers with us. Great Friday always reminds us that we can not imitate his crucifixion. That too would be arrogant. We are the continuing benefactors of his glorious, majestic, triumphal death. We recall a victorious Jesus on a cross in royal and priestly robes with a crown of thorns placed like sunrays surrounding his head and arms outstretched in a loving embrace of a suffering world. Such a cross presents a picture of God's power and glory, not of human defeat at the hands of evil people. Great Friday is a day of sorrow but not of sadness, for in this mysterious death we are able to see the sacrificial love of God delivering the world from the power of evil, through the weakness of power and the power of weakness.

The story of Jesus' death is not the last sad chapter in his life, but rather its climax and indeed the first chapter in the life of humanity. In the words of a sixth-century hymn:

Now above the cross the trophy
Sound the loud triumphal lay,

Tell how Christ the world's redeemer
As a victim won the day.

This is also the story of how God enters our lives and shares our brokenness, our suffering, our distortions of God's image, our dying. In suffering and dying, Christ shares our lives and bears our brokenness so that we might realize we are not alone in our suffering and mortality. Most of us, of course, would prefer to avoid suffering. We become embittered by our crosses. God cares, that we might care for each other. The story of Jesus' death is a story to help us understand that to bear the suffering of others is the way to life.

Near the beginning of Graham Greene's novel *Dr. Fischer of Geneva or the Comb Party* (New York: Simon & Schuster, 1980), two of his characters are talking. One says, "Do you have a soul?" The other responds, "I think so." "Well I'm sure you have a soul!" "How do you know?" "Because you've suffered." To have a soul is to embrace suffering. At an informal family Eucharist I celebrated last year during Lent I asked the group to name persons who they knew were suffering. A little girl sitting next to her father said, "My father's suffering but he will not tell anyone." While I was thinking of a response, she began to hug him. In embarrassment he said, "Oh, Beth, stop, you're going to hug me to death." "No Daddy," she exclaimed, "I'm hugging you to life." And in the human story is the truth of God's Great Friday.

How different the world would appear and how differently we would live if only we could embrace the story of Great Friday. Each week the high point of the Eucharistic prayer comes when we gaze in silence at the re-presentation of Christ's sacrificial life and death enacted in the dramatic breaking of the bread. "Christ our passover is sacrificed for us." Great Friday is the story of the death of Jesus from God's perspective; it is the victory of God not in spite of death but by and through death. The cross has become the tree of life. Our story and God's story once again intersect and the suffering and death we know in our lives and in the world are transformed by the presence of one who shares them with us and empowers us to do likewise on behalf of others.

After a day of solitude, silence, sabbath, God's story continues. It is a story to be told only through the language of poetry, a story only the imagination can comprehend. *Christ is Risen.* The Day of Resurrection has begun. Behind this objectively unverifiable event is the bold conviction that a new world and a new humanity have been born. Human life has taken on a new possibility. We may all live in its light and walk in newness of life. There is in the history of humanity a new beginning.

In a lecture on the resurrection, Harry Wolfson, one of Harvard's great Jewish philosophers, permitted the church fathers to speak for themselves. He imagined that the fathers were still with us and that a bright Harvard student commented to them, "Having been brought up on the wisdom of modern science, I can not possibly accept your story about the resurrection." Professor Wolfson commented, "I imagine the fathers would answer: 'You are mistaken if you think that it is your scientific knowledge that makes it impossible for you to believe this story, for even in our day with our now outmoded science it was impossible to support belief in this story of a resurrection.'" Like the story of the virgin birth, the story of the resurrection is not self-evident: An empty tomb proves nothing; the testimony of folk we never met does little more. Even our own experience can be a delusion. There simply *cannot* be any scientifically verifiable evidence to support God's Easter story; so the fact that there isn't any can be no excuse for our not believing it. Indeed, we cannot expect to find any evidence that will make possible our believing it. Only the eyes of faith can make the invisible visible. Nevertheless, a lot rides on whether or not we have faith in the Easter mystery. What is at stake is everything we believe about God, about human beings, the possibilities of human effort, and the destiny of human history.

God's Easter story is the story of how God acted to make all creation new, to transform humanity, and to redeem the whole world. We are a new people living in a new world. Each person is a new person. Our true condition is as saints, restored in the image of God, reunited with God's Spirit. We may not act accordingly, but that is our sin—the denial of our true condition. The challenge confronting us is to permit God to help us to become who we already are—to actualize the truth about ourselves and to help others actualize and realize the truth about themselves. The world is a new world. God's longed for, hoped for reign has begun. The true condition of our world is justice and peace, freedom and equity, the unity and well-being of all. Evil still exists, of course, but its power is no longer ultimate. Injustice, war, oppression, inequality, division, poverty still exist, but they are a denial of the world's true condition. And so we profess that God's reign has come, is coming, and will come. We live between the already and the not yet, between what is and what is yet to be. The Easter story tells that all is new and that God is always making the new. All of this is less than obvious, but the gift of faith comes to those who gather to reenact the story of God's mighty act in the passion, death, and resurrection of Jesus Christ. In acclaiming these events as true, we enter Eastertide, the most festive season in the church's eternal cycle.

In the early church those who were baptized at the Easter vigil wore white garments and during the week following stood close to the altar for a daily Eucharist and special instruction from the bishop. This period was called the "honeymoon" of their new life in Christ. And so the great fifty days of Easter became the honeymoon season for all Christians. For fifty glorious days we sing and dance, party and celebrate a dream come true, a vision made reality, eternal life in the present.

The stories we tell during this honeymoon season serve as reminders of the realities we will face when the honeymoon is over. The first story we tell is the story of St. Thomas (John 20:19-31). Poor Thomas, nicknamed the doubter, desired only sacrament: an outward and visible sign of the inward and spiritual truth of the resurrection. He didn't doubt the stories told, but he did want some sign, and Jesus gave it to him. Jesus comments, "Blessed are the eyes of the imagination that can see without a sign," but still he offers a sign.

That's the story of our lives, of course. It isn't enough for most of us to be told that someone else loves us. We want that person to do something that expresses love for us. It is a blessing if you can be sustained by love through your imagination, but it surely helps to experience a soft kiss and a gentle hug. So it is with the Easter faith. It's difficult to believe the words, but an action along with the words surely helps. God offers us a word and an action in the sacrament of the Eucharist, and the story of this first week reminds us both of how important that sacrament will be to us after the Easter honeymoon is over and of how we need to be sacrament for the world if others are ever to believe the Easter story. God provides us with sacrament so that we can be sacrament for others.

The next story we come to is about the trip to Emmaus (Luke 24:13-35). It is a story about people haunted by doubts. (Perhaps a bit like honeymooners: What if after this emotional high ends we discover we really don't love each other?) Late on Friday, Jesus was crucified. Saturday was Sabbath, Sunday everything returned to normal. It was all over. They had given up everything for a wild dream, and it had been smashed. All Jesus' promises didn't add up to much. They were wrong. He was not who they thought he was. There were wild rumors that he was alive, but who believes rumors? Get out of town, forget it, head off for Emmaus—a ski weekend to get away from it all, a cocktail party to drown our troubles and hurts, an affair to overcome our doubts about our virility, or even going to church to escape unfulfilled dreams and failures. It's a story we all know. Doubt and skepticism about the Easter faith are simply the human condition. Faced with each evening's news, it's a difficult story to envision, let alone believe. To risk acting as if it were true takes courage. Nevertheless, this story suggests that the gift of the faith to see and the courage to act comes to those who live in a community that has no strangers or estranged people, where God's story is told and everyone shares in a family meal. That may seem unsatisfactory. But we human beings are very odd. All animals eat, but only humans dine, eat with ceremony, and tell stories.

As we begin the fourth week of honeymoon season, our story is about shepherds and sheep (John 10:1-10). It might seem like a strange story unless we consider the temptation of honeymooners. It's easy to escape responsibility, to get lost in each other's embrace, and to live only for each other. "Why can't we live like this forever?" we ask. And that's also the story of God's Easter people. We like knowing that God takes care of us, calls us by name, feeds us, protects us, brings us home, saves us. We celebrate that truth and on any one day would like to keep it for ourselves. We are perfectly happy to be sheep with God as our shepherd. But can we hear the voice of the shepherd calling us to be shepherd for others? "Feed my sheep," Jesus told Peter.

What are sheep like? They get lost, they need constant attention, they can't protect themselves, they will not feed themselves, they're demanding and bothersome. They're like children, the elderly, the terminally ill, those with mental and physical handicaps. They make demands, they sap our energy. God's story reminds us that we too are sheep, God's sheep, and that we have a shepherd to whom we can turn and upon whom we can depend. Because we have a shepherd, we can live interdependent lives and be shepherds to those who need a shepherd. All of which is a good reminder amidst our Easter celebration: When it is over, we will need a shepherd—and we have one; when it is over, we will need to be a shepherd for others—we can't forever live in our honeymoon bliss or only for each other. It isn't enough to love those who love us, to care for those who care for us. We need to care for those who need caring for and we need to be willing to give our lives even for those we do not like, if it will serve their good.

Another week and God's story continues. It's a strange story (John 14:1-21). Jesus says, "Don't be anxious, put your trust in God. You will never be abandoned. Don't worry, there is a first-class room for everyone in God's hotel. I'm showing you the way to God's resort. The pilgrimage, however, is through the harsh realities of life. But stick with it, I promise you it's there."

The honeymoon season is coming to a close and we tell this story to encourage those who will soon return to the mundane existence of daily life. Jesus' message, however, is easy to miss or distort. Some have used this story to convince themselves that because they believe in Jesus, they have a reservation for a private room and bath after death in heaven. Some have used it to support an exclusivist understanding of God's good news—which then becomes bad news for those it condemns to a cell in the subbasement without air conditioning. Nevertheless, what Jesus tries to say in the story is this: Don't be anxious. The honeymoon may be about over, but you can trust me. You are not going to be abandoned. I'm going to have to leave, but I will return in the Holy Spirit to be with you always. Try to understand that. Don't be troubled. Salvation—wholeness and health— are not dependent upon wealth, position, right knowledge or belief, right experience or feeling, right behavior or goodness. It is God's will that everyone enjoy wholeness and health.

Now that is a story of amazing promise concerning the future, but it is not easy to accept it. Our human problem is not that we think too highly of ourselves or have too much confidence in the future, but that we don't think highly enough of ourselves and have little confidence in the future. Too many people believe that there is no health in them and no health in our society. We have accepted depravity and sin as the human condition. We have difficulty believing that we are a redeemed people worthy to stand (not kneel) before the Lord. We need to hear a story of confidence and hope before we return to the trials and tribulations of daily life after the honeymoon.

And so on to the last week and a story that reminds us *to love* (John 15:9-17). A strange reminder for those on a honeymoon? Not really! There is an unreality about honeymoons that makes loving easy. After it is over, the love that seemed so natural can get dull and lifeless. Daily life, most of the time, is not Fantasy Island or the Love Boat. And so God's story reminds us to love. It is a story of special importance, for in our culture we are socialized to believe that our human problem is to be lovable and loved, rather than to love. In pursuit of this aim we strive to be attractive, successful, powerful, and wealthy. We cultivate our bodies, strive to develop pleasant manners, make interesting conversation, acquire a host of hobbies, get a good education and a lucrative job. Being attractive means having a nice package of qualities in the physical-personality market. Two persons fall in love when they feel they have found the best object available on the market, considering the limitations of their own exchange value. And, of course, when they find something better, they seek an easy quick exchange.

Our culture socializes us to treat one another as things, things to possess. *To have* has replaced *to be* in our conversations. We say we *have* a friend, a mate, a home, a job, children, degrees. While there are the unabashed *eros* of lovers who serve each other's needs and the sympathetic *philia* of friends who share common interests, the love our story calls us to is the *agape* of charity that gives itself away freely no less to the criminal than to the criminal's victim. To lose ourselves in another's embrace or in another's company is one thing, but to lose ourselves in suffering with those who suffer, or even with those who inflict suffering on us, is another. Our story calls us to a love that is not an idea or an emotion, but an act of the will on behalf of another's well-being, even if that means sacrificing our own.

God's sacrificial love for us has been demonstrated in the mystery of Christ's passion and death and resurrection. When we were most unlovable, God revealed passionate love for us so that we, being so loved, might be able to love the unlovable and the unloved. So our human story of needing to be loved without merit and God's story of gracious love for each of us intersect. As we have lost ourselves in that love during our Easter honeymoon season, we are reminded to share that love with the whole world. So God's story and our stories go on. Eastertide comes to a close and a new season begins.

Three

Life in the Spirit

Eastertide draws to a close, the party season of the church's eternal cycle has ended, the honeymoon is over. Ascension Day has arrived and in Mark 16:9-20 the story takes a dramatic change. Jesus in essence said to his disciples, "You are now me, but without spirit." To the church he says, "You are my body, but you are impotent." Perhaps only those who have wanted children more than anything in this world but have been unable to have them can really understand the feelings related to this day. Yet each of us has experienced impotence of one sort or another, especially the seeming lack of power to realize fully our human potential or make the world a better place. Powerlessness is a common experience. The story ends, however, with a promise that the spirit of potency, God's life-giving spirit, will come. "Do not despair; wait in trust; the Holy Spirit is coming. You will yet be potent. God will make you persons of power. I am returning to God, you will be my body, my presence in the world. You may wonder how you will ever be able to be that, but contemplate what that may mean for you while you wait. I will send the Spirit, the life-giving power necessary for you to be me. Live in that Spirit and one day I will return again and unite you with myself" (John 14:26 ff.).

The story rings so very true. We have sung and danced even amidst evil days because we have believed that God has made possible a new heaven and a new earth. Then we have once again become conscious of the fact that we are to do more than celebrate the good news, we are to manifest it and bring its hope to life for people. Amidst that awareness we are confronted by the fact that we have come nowhere near achieving that potential in our lives or in the life of the church. We experience a sense of impotency. We admit that on our own we simply do not have the power to be who we really are. Our human problem is that we get lost in our own strivings; we begin to think that we can change the world, that we can be something and make an important contribution to society all by ourselves. And then comes the awareness that we cannot pull it off by ourselves. This is where our story and God's story of Ascension Day intersect. It is one thing to celebrate Christ in glory; it is another to realize that we are to be his presence here on earth. It is one thing to celebrate God's power; it is another to realize our powerlessness.

And then comes the Sunday after Ascension Day and the story of what Jesus' first followers did between Jesus' ascension and the coming of God's Spirit (John 17:1-26). It's a story that helps us to understand what we must do and how we must live if we are to receive the gift of potency. First, they stayed and waited for the Lord. They faced up to their inability to do anything alone and prayed that God's spirit might enter their lives and empower them to be what they already were. They began to look for the One who was to come. In short, they set themselves apart to wait in prayer. They aimed to be holy. We too need to become holy: to wait and pray for the mighty action of God in our time, always faithful in prayer and expectation.

Second, they stayed together. Jesus' prayer for them had been "That they all might be one." There was to be no wrangling or dissension. They were of one accord, not claiming more and thinking more highly of themselves than of others. They were one. We too need to become one. Wrangling and dissension need to be healed. Inequalities and separations between men and women, clergy and laity, rich and poor, wise and foolish must be abolished. Our corporate life needs to encompass mutual trust, understanding, affirmation, and self-sacrifice.

Third, their oneness was not an artificial unity, a conglomerate of diverse people tolerating each other or a conglomerate of folk in which everyone loses identity and is absorbed into a single undifferentiated whole. No, they remained individuals, a diverse group with distinct personalities each unique in his or her own ways. We too need to become fully catholic. We must maintain both a common identity and personality. We must encourage diversity so that all the gifts present in people can shine. The church is catholic: inclusive of the world's diversity, each person maintaining uniqueness and sharing gifts with all the others for their common benefit.

And last, for the Holy Spirit to come, they had to accept responsibility for being Christ's body in the world. We do need to accept honestly the call to be apostolic, that is, so to live that when people look at us, the church, they will see a sign of God's reign in society. They will see a people who believe that God's will can be accomplished in this world.

Of course, behind this story on the Sunday after Ascension Day is the assumption that we are communal beings. To be part of the body of Christ is to be in the church. One Christian is no Christian. When, however, did you last hear any radio evangelists try to convert souls to Christ and his church? Typically, these evangelists strive to convert souls to Christ alone. Other people (often those who rarely participate in the church's life) desire private baptisms and believe that this privatized action saves the child's soul. God's story gives us a different vision of life. One way we share this vision in the life of the church is with the kiss of peace. Many persons have difficulty with the kiss of peace because it seems so intimate, so communal. And this is exactly what it intends to be, for it tries to proclaim that in the church there are no strangers and no estranged people. God's story on the Sunday following Ascension Day reminds us of the communal nature of the Christian faith and life. That's a lot to accept, but—says the story—unless we do, we can never be the body of Christ with power.

So it is that Pentecost becomes the story of both the gift of

God's Spirit of potency and the birthday of the church (John 20:19-23). At Pentecost, God's promised Spirit came to the Church. Christ's body was brought to life and empowered to know and do God's will.

Walter Brueggemann, biblical scholar and friend, wrote an essay based on my book *Will Our Children Have Faith?*. He entitled it "Will Our Faith Have Children?" by which he meant, Will we be open enough, risking enough, vulnerable enough that God may give us a future that we do not plan or control or contrive? Are we able to acknowledge our impotency so that we might receive from God the gift of a future that surprises us? Each year between Ascension and Pentecost we remember that we are a community of barren men and unproductive women (Hebrews 11:12) with no possibility of creating a future of our own, but that it is precisely to the barren ones that God makes the promise of fertility. It is a nonsensical idea unless it is taken as evangelical, that is, as a reason for hope against the reason of the day. It is not a glib hope of self-denial without grief and despair. We want to rush too easily to a bright tomorrow. The story of Pentecost is true, but only to those who take Ascension Day seriously. Unless we weep, utterly bereft, on Ascension Day, we cannot sing, utterly stunned, on Pentecost. However, if we do, then God's Spirit frees us from despair, hopelessness, and helplessness; it shakes us from our complacency and renews our visions and hopes. Though we speak many languages, God's Spirit invites us in a common call to live for justice, peace, and righteousness. The body is given life, the church is born, and we in the church celebrate our potency: life in the Spirit. Pentecost is a day for baptisms, the adoption and incorporation of new life into the Church, and the renewal of our baptismal covenant imbuing us with God's Spirit that we might fulfill our vows. As believers in Jesus Christ and members of his church (those who have faith in the Paschal mystery and have been marked as Christ's own forever), we are called to live in the Spirit—to live in relationship to God, self, neighbor, and the natural world—to the end that God's will be done and God's reign come.

This brings us to the close of God's story—the story of God entering into human history to redeem the world through the life, death, and resurrection of Jesus Christ and God entering the world to form and empower the church to witness to that redemption through the presence of the Holy Spirit. But before we move from this story—the story that shapes our lives and gives them meaning and purpose—to the season of ordinary time, in which we explore the implications of God's story for our personal and corporate life, we celebrate Trinity Sunday. Since the whole story is about God, we take this one Sunday each year to remember the image of God revealed in God's story. This is important, for as Jesus' story of the talents makes very clear, the God we image is the God we get (Matthew 25:14-30). Recall the story: The first two servants envisioned God as loving, caring, and affirming. God trusted them and gave them freedom to manifest God's image in their lives, but would not forsake or punish them if they failed. They acted accordingly, and God proved to be just such a loving, caring, affirming God. But the third servant envisioned God as harsh, judgmental, unforgiving. God would punish him if he messed up, and in the story that is exactly what God does. We get what we image.

And so before we enter those days of living as the presence of God in the world that encompass one-half the church's year, it is good to remind ourselves who God is. The Trinity reminds us that God is a communal being: three persons yet one, the holy and undivided Trinity. The implication should be clear: We in the image of God are intended to be communal persons as well. God lives in community and as a communal being manifests God's self as creator, redeemer, and perfecter. The problems created by the mystery of the Trinity, however, are great; and each year on this occasion it is good for the church to bring them to the surface.

We want to avoid the erroneous idea that God is only masculine or two-thirds masculine (Father-Son). In monotheistic religions, God tends to be masculine; in polytheistic religions, God tends to be feminine. The doctrine of the Trinity makes possible the notion of an androgynous god in which the equality of women and men as persons finds expression. Still the formulation—Father, Son, and Holy Spirit—makes that difficult to envision. To move to God as creator, redeemer, and perfecter causes other problems that are yet to be resolved.

Nevertheless, on this transition Sunday in our journey through time in a story-formed community, it is good for us to remind ourselves that we are an androgynous people living in community; that is, we are people in the image of God, called and empowered to be a creative people, a redemptive people, perfecters of human life and history. All of this implies that the preservation of life, human and natural, is to be normative. Similarly, creativity is to be enhanced and enlivened. The liberation of life from all that oppresses is also normative. Racism, sexism, classism, nationalism, or any other social evil that prevents wholeness and holiness of all life is to be overcome. Finally, the realization of peace and justice, unity and well-being of all humanity is normative. All the world living in harmony and for common ends is our goal.

For those ends God lives. We, women and men bound together in community in the image of God, are to do likewise, for that is what it means to live in the Spirit.

Four

Ordinary Days and Ways

Moving from one depth or peak experience to another can be either exhilarating or exhausting, but it is always exciting. Ordinary days can be mundane and at times tiring, but they are rarely exciting. Still, in the eternal cycle they are as essential as the great feasts and fasts, and in significant ways they are the test of how faithfully we have celebrated the rest of the year. During one-half of each year we explore the implications of Easter and endeavor to live into our baptism. The stories told through this season are numerous and diverse. To catch the spirit of this time I have selected only a few at random, with the principle of diversity in mind.

For example, there is the story told by Jesus about seeds sown and the growth of God's kingdom (Matthew 13:24-32). The story explains that the seeds of God's reign have been planted and that we can be confident a harvest will follow. Its growth, however, will be a mystery. But no matter how bad things look, don't give up, keep the faith and act in hope.

Related to this story is another, a parable or story intended to subvert the ways we normally see things so we can see them properly. It is a story about a mustard seed that becomes a huge bush. Our culture socializes us to believe that only big things matter; but in God's world, says this story, small acts make a big difference. I recall a friend telling about her experience while attending a conference on the future. A very somber and sober academic was outlining the chances of the world's survival to the year 2000, if we continued as we were going. It was a very bleak picture; when he finished there was no applause, just deep silence. An old woman in the back of the room stood up and said, "I'm not sure I heard or understood all you said but it sounded urgent and I'm sure it calls for each of us to do something. But I don't know what to say or do. Would it help if I baked a cake?" Everyone laughed, but the old woman looked hurt. She was not trying to be funny, and she didn't think she was innocent. "I think," said my friend, "that, she was testifying amidst the silence to her trust in God and to her conviction that any act done faithfully makes some difference." Even in these days of the apocalypse we can have hope and give the little bit we've got, perform those small but faithful acts where we live, and have faith that in the mystery of life in the Spirit they will make a difference.

Ordinary time may lack the drama of Jesus' life, death, and resurrection, but it more than makes up for it in the drama of his teachings about how our lives are to be lived faithfully.

For example, in another story Jesus reminds us of the fact that where our treasure is, there is our heart also (Matthew 6:21). Interestingly, I don't know many people who really believe it. Many persons work on the hypothesis that if we could only get people to believe the gospel, they would behave as Christians; if we could only convince them that the gospel is true, they would live accordingly. Others are sure that if only people would have some particular religious experience, a conversion, they would act as Christians. No, says Jesus, it works the other way around. It's not where we put our hearts that we find our treasure. Rather, we are much more likely to act our way into a new way of thinking than to think our way into a new way of acting. We make love to fall in love. We make believe to believe. So ordinary time serves the rest of the church year, for in living the faithful life we come to faith; by living as an Easter people we perceive the truth of Easter and experience its word of new life. For truly, where our treasure is, there are our hearts and minds also.

Then there is the story of the woman who came and sat at Jesus' feet, washing them with her tears, and of Jesus' host who had trouble understanding unearned, undeserved love and the living of a Eucharistic life (Luke 7:36-50). The more we mess up, the more God forgives. God loves us in spite of anything we might do. There is nothing we can do for which God will not forgive us; there is nothing we need do to deserve God's love. God finds us lovable no matter how we act. God loves us because we need to be loved and not because we deserve to be loved. If we could only understand that, we would all live a Eucharistic life in gratitude to God.

Recall the story of a private conversation between Jesus and his students (Matthew 16:13-20). Jesus asked, "You know what others are saying, but who do you think that I am?" Their response could have been, "We don't know, we're not sure," or they could simply have agreed with any of the identities others attributed to him. But impulsive, intuitive Peter responded, "You are the one who will save us." That is, you will fulfill the world's hope for wholeness and health and fullness of life. And Jesus said, "Do you realize that I will do that by identifying with and embracing the world's brokenness, sickness, and suffering?" And then he added, "If you want your hopes for true life fulfilled, you will need to do the same." It may appear as if the best way to have life, freedom, and happiness is to avoid the world's brokenness, sickness, and suffering; but the truth is just the opposite.

Then there is the story of Jesus explaining, "You have heard it said that you must not kill, but I say to you do not nurse anger . . ." (not "do not be angry," as some read it) (Matthew 5:21-24). Do not nurse anger. Do not let the sun set on your anger. Be angry, but do not sin. And Jesus continued, "If you are going to make your offering and anyone is angry with you" (not, as many read it, "if you are angry with someone") "first be reconciled by bringing him or her my peace." There is nothing wrong with being angry, but we must not nurse it. If someone is angry with us, it is our responsibility to strive for reconciliation. It all seems practical and obvious enough, but we need to be reminded, or at least it seems that we do. We have difficulty dealing with our anger. We repress our anger or we stay angry forever, and when someone in or outside the church is angry with us, we think it is her or his responsibility to do something about it. Forgiveness and reconciliation are difficult even among persons in the church.

Luke also tells a story of a lawyer who asked, "What do I need to do to gain eternal life?" (Luke 10:25-37). Jesus said, "Love God and love your neighbor." And then Jesus told a story about a man who was attacked by robbers. A priest walked by, but not because he did not care. The religious law stated that a priest could not make contact with anyone who had died. If he had gone to the man and the man was dead or died in his presence, his career would have been finished. Similarities should come to mind. If a priest today takes a stand on certain issues or performs acts that violate the people's mores (ethical or not), he or she could lose effectiveness as a priest, or perhaps worse, be removed from responsibility. The Levite had a different problem. He was due at the temple to help with the religious ceremonies. If he got detained, he too might lose his job. Again the analogies. If we stop to help "the drunken bum who has stolen a typewriter from the church" and thereby do not show up to care for the needs of those who employ us, we have endangered our jobs. But in Jesus' story it was the Samaritan, the one who had nothing to lose, who could afford to stop and care. And that's the key to the story. We need to learn, explains Jesus, to live as if we have nothing to lose; then and only then can we truly love our neighbor, who is anyone and everyone in need.

There is another story about two sons (Matthew 21:28-32). The one says yes and then doesn't act; the other says no but does. Interestingly, there are no characters in the story who say yes and do it or no and do not, so the story cannot be about doing what you say or being honest. The story is rather about God desiring our capacity to say no. Only if we do God's will freely (not because of duty or fear of authority) is it a moral act. The story also reminds us that holiness and right action are synonymous. Piety and politics, the material and the spiritual, are united in Jesus' understanding of wholeness of life or salvation. And so Jesus taught, "Holy are they who depend on God alone; holy are those who identify with the poor, the hungry, the oppressed, and the needy; holy are those who act for the liberation and reconciliation of humanity; holy are those who generously care for every human need; holy are those who acknowledge that everything comes from God and nothing belongs to them; holy are those who have a passion for justice and peace; and holy are those who are willing to pay any price so the good of humanity might be achieved" (Matthew 5:3 ff.).

Jesus in another story explained, "I have not come to bring peace but a sword" (Matthew 10:34-42). What could he possibly mean? Is this a justification for violence? True, Jesus comes and brings a sword, but the sword is not in Jesus' hand. Rather, it is because Jesus comes that a sword appears. And that sword appears in the hands of the worldly, those set against Jesus. Jesus is the sign of goodness; the sword is a sign of the evil that comes to destroy goodness. Jesus continued in this story to remind his followers that he is apt to cause divisions in families as well. Any true follower of Jesus will learn the piercing anguish of a conflict of loyalty between those whom he or she loves and the master we must love most of all. Following Jesus means taking up a cross, which is just another way of saying that the world will put to the sword anyone bold enough to dare to speak the good news of love in a sinful and selfish world. Jesus reminds us that the world's way is the sword. But those who take the sword will suffer from alienation, violence, and death; indeed they will perish by the sword. On the other hand, those who abandon the sword for God's way, which is love, will know the pain of the sword, be crucified, stoned, beheaded, imprisoned, shunned, disowned; but they will be raised up in victory.

In another story some students came up to Jesus and said, "We know that you know the truth and you teach the ways of God faithfully, so would you be kind enough to give us an opinion? Is it lawful to give taxes to Caesar or not?" (Matthew 22:15-22). Now that is one of those trick questions to which any answer you give is wrong. Unwilling to play the game, Jesus took a coin and asked, "Where did you get this?" "From the government," they responded. "Fine," said Jesus, "since it really doesn't belong to you, why don't you return it? Return it to the state because that is where it came from." Then Jesus said, "Now my friends, the important question: Where did you get your life?" "From God." "Good, now go and give it back to God, since that is where it came from." And as you might guess, that ended the conversation.

In one story after another Jesus tried to teach his students to ask the right questions. In this case, the right question is not, "What do we owe the state?" but "What do we owe God?" At our baptism we were given a new life and were branded with a cross so that we might never forget and the world might always know to whom we belong. As we celebrate the Eucharist each week we are subtly reminded to give our lives back to God; the offertory is our opportunity to do this. That is also why we celebrate the death days of the martyrs and call them heroes. Like the lives of the martyrs who followed his example, Jesus' life was one of downward mobility and sacrificial death. To our upwardly mobile society that cannot help but be a radical, subversive idea, a jarring and unsettling challenge. Yet somewhere deep in our hearts we know that success, titles, fame, influence, possessions, power, knowledge, wealth, and even achievements do not give us the inner joy and peace we crave. There is no way to escape it: The downward way, the way of the cross, is God's way to joy, peace, and life. And so, as pilgrims on the way to wholeness and holiness, we come each week to be reminded of what the Lord requires—the sacrifice of our lives.

The weeks go on. We bring our stories with us and listen

to the stories Jesus told about what it means to live as children of God. During the year we also celebrate a host of holy days: Holy Innocents (Dec. 28), the Confession of St. Peter (Jan. 18), the Conversion of St. Paul (Jan. 25), the Annunciation (Mar. 25), the Nativity of St. John the Baptist (June 24), the Transfiguration (Aug. 6), Holy Cross Day (Sept. 14), St. Michael and All Angels (Sept. 29), and All Saints' Day (Nov. 1). Each brings together a piece of God's story and our stories. On the eve of the Nativity of St. John the Baptist, we tell the story of Zechariah who had a vision: An angel came to him bearing the news that he would become a parent. Because of his unbelief he was speechless, but Elizabeth had the baby (Luke 1:57-80). We never know for sure what God will do. We never know for sure the particularity of God's will. All we know is that when God acts, it will be for our benefit. God speaks in visions and dreams. In our day it is not that we do not believe them, but that we don't see them. Our problem is not being speechless following a vision, but being blind to visions. We need to learn to live in expectation, to open ourselves to a revelation of God's will.

On All Saints' Day we celebrate baptisms and remind ourselves and each other that we are all saints. Perhaps there is no more important day to celebrate than All Saints', since so few see the saint in themselves or in others. And unless we see it we will never act as saints or be contrite when we do not. I recall an evening in class a year ago. Since the class meets in the evening and includes a number of single parents, they often bring their children to class. One evening a six year old interrupted me and said, "Next week is my birthday." "Would you like a party?" I asked. "Sure," she shouted, with joy showing all over her body. "What kind of party would you like?" And she answered, "A party where everyone is a king or queen." The next week a group of children arrived before class. We made scepters, crowns, and a cake. When we gathered I told them that each of us was supposed to imagine that walking in front of us and everyone we meet was a host of angels shouting, "Make way for the image of God! Make way for the image of God!" (As Charles Williams, the English author, says, if everyone did that, everyone would walk with their head high and fall in love with everyone they meet.) We set those words to music, dressed up, and went parading through the divinity school singing, "Make way for the image of God!" After the party was over, the birthday girl gave me a hug and said, "That's the best party I have ever had. I wish everyone could be a king or queen every day." "They could, you know," I responded, "if only we could learn to make believe." We celebrate All Saints' Day to remind ourselves that we are saints of God and if only we could really make believe, it just might be real as well as true. You see, sin is not our natural human condition. Sainthood is. Sin is the denial of the truth about ourselves. And the achievement of sainthood is simply being who we already are. While we may not act as saints, we are saints and called to be saints; and so on this day we do not concentrate on spiritual heroes, but on people who are saints by loving each other, suffering with each other, caring for one another, and forgiving one another in their natural everyday lives. Throughout the year, in a host of lesser feasts and fasts, we tell stories of how God's story has intersected with the stories of others who exemplified some particular trait of sainthood so that we can see that same potential within ourselves: John Chrysostom, Thomas Aquinas, Ignatius of Loyola, Martin Luther, John and Charles Wesley, Absalom Jones, Gregory the Great, F. D. Maurice, William Law, Monica, Augustine, St. Nicholas, and many others.

Eventually we reach the last Sunday in ordinary time. Advent approaches and we celebrate the festival of Christ the King. This long season in which we have struggled to discern and do the will of God, to live faithfully as believers of Jesus Christ and members of his church, comes to a close on a note of visionary universalism. In Jesus Christ God did something for all humanity, not just for Christians. The church can never become a self-conscious, self-righteous private club for the saved. No one need do anything to receive the benefits of God's salvation. We can only use our freedom to deny the gift. As Christians we ought to hope and pray with God that none will deny the gift, but rather that each in a unique way will come to know the gift of God's love, and so live joyfully and thankfully in its grace. God's story explains that we have been called so to live that all others may know what is true for them also. The church and its sacraments are not the only doorways to God's grace. They celebrate our awareness of that grace and so make it more real but not more true. Our mission is not to give people something they do not have, but to help them to see what they already do have, so that they may choose to live in such a way that others will also know. We come to church because its story helps us to make sense of our stories. Through the season of ordinary time the stories told inspire us to pray that we may be worthy of our calling; that we may be inspired to do God's will; that we may minister with justice and compassion; that we may live in unity and have our weaknesses overcome; that we may be a peaceable people; that we may do good works and reveal God's power; that we may have confidence in God's gifts and God may rule in our hearts; that we may hold fast to what endures and run the race without struggling; and that we may love what God commands and acknowledge God's rule over all.

And the stories we tell help us to understand how our lives might best be lived so that our stories might manifest God's story.

Throughout ordinary time we tell stories and explore their implications for our lives as God's stewards, fruitful trustees of God's gifts and graces. Stewardship, properly understood, is nothing less than a complete lifestyle, a total accountability and responsibility before God. Stewardship is what we do after we say we believe, that is, after we give our love, loyalty, and trust to God, from whom every aspect of our lives comes as a gift. As members of God's household, we are subject to God's economy, that is, God's plan to redeem and reconcile the whole world and bring creation to its proper end. Ordinary time helps us to understand the implications of stewardship and worship: praise and thanksgiving to the One to whom we have pledged love and loyalty; proclamation in word and deed, by how we act toward the natural world and all humanity, especially those denied God's gifts—the poor, hungry, and dispossessed; the acquisition and use of our wealth and possessions for the benefit of all peoples; the recognition and use of our talents and skills in the service of others; the nonviolent use of power on behalf of justice and peace; support for the work of the church, shown by the style of our institutional life, our priorities and programs, and our use of the church's material and human resources.

But six months of ordinary, mundane life is tiring. The long, hard work of living into our baptism begins to lose its vitality. The dream fades; the vision dulls; we get weary in well-doing. God's story has slowly and gradually receded from our consciousness. A change is needed—and it comes.

Five

Recapturing Lost Visions

Once again ordinary time draws to a close. Aware of global estrangement, brokenness, and despair—and conscious of the emptiness and poverty in our own lives—we whisper, Thank God. Another year has ended; we have grown older together, but our visions and dreams have grown dimmer. Nostalgia for the past has replaced hope for the future. We are anxious about the present and weary in well-doing. We wish we had a clearer picture of what God has still to accomplish in and through us. However, just as we feel trapped in cyclical feelings of having lost faith in the Easter mystery, Advent comes once again. Perhaps best understood through the metaphor of pregnancy, Advent offers us a word of hope, the possibility of birthing new life, a rekindled vision to which we might give our lives. It is not so much a penitential season focused on our unfaithfulness as it is a season of paradoxes: longing anticipation and patient watching; transforming the way we envision life and yet living prepared; living out a wait for what never seems to come and continuing in hopeful trust; desiring to give up control and opening ourselves to new possibilities for life. All of these are responses to God's unmerited and gracious love for us, God's implanting of life in us at the very moment in our lives when we have grown weary and have lost hope.

Perhaps if we really took seriously these stories of Advent, life in the church would be somewhat different from what most of us know it to be. For many of us, Advent is preparation for a secular Christmas through frantic, exhausting escapist behavior. We eat too much, party too much, stay up too late. And when Christmas comes, we fall apart. We frantically decorate and clean our homes. We buy presents. By the end of Advent some have experienced what they call "Christmas joy," but it is short-lived and lacking in depth. It is a season when the lonely tend to experience greater loneliness, the broken have their wounds opened again, the weary end up more tired, and everyone is poorer. Few experience a second coming, a rebirth of new life, and the presence of that peace, hope, healing, love, joy promised to those who need them most. If the church is to be a gift to those whose lives cry out for good news, it will need to rethink how it integrates the stories of people with its story during the Advent season. This in turn will mean reflecting more deeply on the stories of Advent and more honestly on the stories of our lives.

With the kindling of the first flame of Advent, we mark an ending and a beginning to the eternal cycle, the sacred story of God intended to illumine and make sense of our profane history. Most of us are weary of the long season of ordinary time and are ready for a change. Still, Advent is a season to be grasped only in the language of poetry. It opens with a reminder to be alert, to watch, to live in a state of constant anticipation. That is not easy. We want things to happen now. It seems as though all we do is wait. Who can sustain a lifetime of vigilance, of watching for what never seems to come?

Each year we proclaim that what we desire is near, but it often seems that what we hope for is ever further away. We watch for war to end and peace to come; for oppression to end and freedom to come; for inequality to end and justice to come; for estrangement to end and reconciliation to come; for poverty, hunger, and sickness to end and health to come; for hatred to end and love to come; for death to end and life to come. It is difficult to believe that all these will ever come. So, in this profane season of canned music, store-window fairyland, presents, mistletoe, and spiked punch, we are tempted to escape the depression of unfulfilled watching. It is easier to give up looking and get on with

-44-

living the best we can. Still, on the first Sunday of the church's new year we gather to remind ourselves that the object of our anticipation is not a fantasy, but a reality ever available to the imagination, ever near to the eyes of faith, even though yet to come. The story of Advent is that we are to watch for the coming of what has already come. Jesus tells over and over again the story of God's coming reign and he gives the same advice: Take heed and watch, for while you will not know when, you can be sure that it will occur. Therefore, be ready (Mark 13:33-37).

As Christians, we live between the already and the not yet. We celebrate Advent in the light of Easter. Thus we live a life of watchful anticipation between two comings: God's coming in Jesus—a Jewish baby, born to Mary and Joseph, who grew up to suffer under the Roman government and be crucified and raised from the dead—and God's second coming in the crucified-resurrected Christ. To the question "When?" God only answers, "Watch, tomorrow may be the day." Are we ready? Are we even looking? Or have we decided that this is the best of all possible worlds and settled down to accept life as it is? It is easy to become numb to the world's evil, to give in to our own brokenness. Instead of being vigilant, we prepare for the long haul by making the best of a mundane life in what we consider to be an evil world among evil people. Having lost the memory and the vision of the Easter story, we live in the present as if that is all there is. Would it make any difference in our personal lives and in the life of the church if we really anticipated the fulfillment of God's promise and set about watching for the signs of its coming?

Dietrich Bonhoeffer spent the winter of 1943 in prison. On the first morning of Advent, following a frightening night of bombing he arose, prayed, and hung a wreath on his prison wall. His biographer writes, "He could look around him on Advent morning and see the ruins to which Christ must come again." Advent is a season of realism, not of escape. No tinsel glitter and shining balls, no hiding from reality, but facing the world and ourselves as we have distorted them, ever watching for the signs of where Christ is trying to break in.

And so God's story during the first week in Advent advises us to watch in anticipation, to be vigilant and open to the mystery of God's second coming.

The musical *Godspell* made popular our second Advent theme, "Prepare ye the way of the Lord" (Mark 1:1-8). As a second flame is kindled in the Advent wreath, we are invited to listen to the story about a voice ever crying in the wilderness, calling us to live prepared. "But how are we to do that?" we ask. And our story records John the baptizer as saying, "Change the way you see things."

To repent is to change our perception, to recognize that the reign of God is at hand, that life in the world to come has already begun. To repent is not to lament our sins or be sorry for evil we've done; it is to have faith, to perceive life and our lives in a new way. We need to be converted over and over again in our human pilgrimage, for we keep losing the vision.

For too long we have surrendered to the illusion that nurture alone will rekindle the fire of faith. We have expected too much of nurture. Conversions are a necessary part of the process of Christian life. The repentance to which a Christian is called is a continuous, lifelong process affecting every aspect of our lives. While conversion begins, as everything in history does, at some point in time, the process of conversion is not complete until every aspect of the human personality is driven out into the light of God's grace and transformed. Conversions proceed layer by layer, relationship by relationship, a little here and a little there, until the whole personality is re-created by God. Advent is a time to open ourselves to those transforming moments.

As the third flame is kindled, the story tells of a group of people who came to John and asked, "Who are you?" (John 1:6-8, 19-68). He answered: "I'm not Christ, I'm not Elijah, I'm not a prophet—I'm just a voice crying, 'Get ready, wait patiently in hope.'" Wait in hope, hope in God, believing that we already possess what we hope for. In this season of sacred quiet amidst profane noise; of sacred, patient calmness amidst profane frantic rushing; of sacred contemplation amidst profane activity; of sacred fasting amidst profane feasting—we who have been baptized into new life experience ourselves as strangers in a strange land. We find ourselves drawn away from the tinsel and carols of our profane world into the sanctuary of sacred time and space, where we might learn what it means to wait for the coming of what has already come. In the words of Flannery O'Connor, "I think the Church is the only thing that can make our terrible world endurable and the only thing that makes the Church endurable is that it is somehow the Body of Christ and on that we feed" (*The Habit of Being: Letters of Flannery O'Connor,* New York: Vintage Books, 1980, p. 90). It is in the sacraments that the mystery of past and future is made present, the invisible made visible. "Now as always it is in the area of liturgics that our main impasse lies, for it is at the level of the imagination that the fateful issues of our life experience must first be mastered," wrote Amos Wilder, the poet and New Testament scholar (from the Foreword to *Grace Confounding: Poems by Amos Wilder,* Philadelphia: Fortress Press, 1972). Out of our separateness we join together in a holy meal of sacred memories and anticipations, so that the present moment of lost dreams, sorrows and hurts, unfulfilled desires, frustrated hopes, and ever-present anxieties might be transformed, and so that we might be given a clearer glimpse of all that has come, is coming, and will come.

It is difficult to wait in hope. Yet Advent provides us with a moment to reflect on where Christ is trying to break into our lives and into our world. It is time to ask, Are we watching, are we expecting, are we ready to see it? Do we really want it to come?

It is so easy to forget. Christ has been born. We do not need to prepare for the birth of Jesus. In Advent we are reminded that we are to live prepared, prepared for Christ's second coming. We know what is to come; it's a new heaven and a new earth, God's surprising future. It is almost two thousand years since Jesus was born and recognized by some as savior of the world. We do not prepare for that birth. Of course, at Christmas we remember that birth, but only so that we will not forget the vision of a new possibility he implanted in our hearts and the promise of his return upon which we base our hope and for which we watch in constant anticipation. It is not the birth of a baby, but Christ's coming again that is the proper focus of our Advent waiting.

As a fourth light is kindled, the last week in this season of pregnancy has come, and we hear the story of an angel coming to Mary. "The Lord is with you," the angel said (Luke 1:26-38). As you might suspect, this is a confusing and troubling message: "Who me? Why me? What do you mean?" said Mary. "Don't be afraid," said the angel. The first thing the angels always say is, "The Lord be with you," and the second is, "Don't be afraid." It is awesome to be in the presence of God! "You are going to conceive and bear a son and call him Jesus, the one who saves." And as we might guess, she asked, "How is that going to be possible?" And the answer was simple, "Nothing is impossible with God." And Mary, giving up all control, responded, "So be it!"

Now that's not easy to do. Most of us want to control. We want to make things happen. But as Nikos Kazantzakis writes, "Our profound human duty is not to interpret or cast light on the rhythm of God's march, it is to adjust as much as we can the rhythm of our small fleeting life to him" (*The Saviors of God*, New York: Simon & Schuster, 1960, p. 107). Recently I was directing a priest on retreat. He had come with great expectations. But two days had passed and nothing had happened. He had worked hard at his praying and knew that he had only one day left. Frustration set in. I had watched it happen before. Some just give up, some get angry at the retreat director, some go off and escape with a few drinks. I said to him, "Perhaps you are trying to manipulate the relationship. God wants us to let go, to stop working so hard at prayer. God must be the Lord of this relationship. We cannot turn God on and off like a water faucet whenever we are ready. Prayer is like learning to float. Our natural impulse is to want to do something, but the only way to float is to give up that instinct and relax so that the water can hold us up. The secret is in learning not to do all the things we think we must do to save ourselves. When we learn to rest on the water, to give up control, then we understand the mystery of Advent."

The Lord is coming, always coming. Advent—a season of watching in anticipation, of living prepared, of waiting in hope, of giving up control—draws to a close. Christmas—the birth of a possibility, a candle in the dark—approaches, and we remember Mary, the Blessed Virgin, the mother of God. We remember that we are called to be like Mary, to open ourselves, to make ourselves vulnerable, to be pregnant with God. She offers us courage to be the handmaidens of God. Her virginity gives us hope, for in her we see how God creates out of nothing. Like Mary we can be God's lover, we can make ourselves available to be used for God's purposes. Through her we learn to admit that new life is not limited to our doing. To our weakness she offers us faith to be the instruments of God's life-giving love.

And so Advent closes. "Something's Coming," as the song from *West Side Story* puts it. Advent is a season of quiet reflection, of solitude and silence, of meditation and prayer: a time to slow down the hectic pace of life and get in touch with our longings, hopes, and dreams; a time to wait and prepare for the birth of possibilities by cleaning out the clutter of our busy lives and decorating hospitable space for the birth of new life; a time to pay attention to the pain in our gut, to care for our bodies, minds, and spirits with the faith that what we experience going on inside us is a pregnancy and not a malignancy. If the church does not provide that space and encourage those activities, who will? The story of our lives needs the story of Advent—if only we can free ourselves from its secular distortions.

Six

The Birth of Possibilities

Christmas as a season in the Christian year may to some seem a lost cause. What energy is left after our typical frantic pre-Christmas festivities? The persons on the *New York Times* "Neediest" list have had their troubles dulled for the moment. Kind deeds have been done, but their problems remain. Money has been contributed to help people, but the social evils that cause their need remain. Caught up in the nostalgia of the Christmas spirit, we try to make up for neglect and ineptitude, but in a couple of weeks the Christmas decorations put up before Thanksgiving will be torn down and little will have substantially changed. Nevertheless, Christmastide—best understood through the metaphor of birth—brings God to us in the midst of our distortions.

Christmas is a time in the eternal cycle to celebrate the mystery of possibilities through the birth of a child. The story is all too familiar (Luke 2:1-20). A birth is a joyful occasion, but it is also a sobering and sometimes a sorrowful moment. There are children born whose possibilities seem so limited: children with physical and mental disabilities. Even the birth of a healthy child causes moments of anxiety. A child represents possibilities, but no certainty. Shortly after birth the child might be seriously injured or die; in childhood, besides physical danger there is the risk of psychological trauma, culminating in adolescence with the risk of suicide. All too often Christmas offers people nostalgia, an escape from the harsh realities of life, rather than the joy-filled experience of new possibilities—but only possibilities—amidst the realities of personal life and world history. The Christmas spirit is not a drug to numb our senses but a moment to recall that with God everything is possible. In Advent we wait quietly in hope for dreams that grow dim with age. At Christmas we experience the eternal promise of new possibilities. We are birthed again in our hearts and in our history, because of our faith that God has entered human history and become one with us.

God came and comes to us at Christmas because God wants to join us on our journey so that we will never have to fear or feel lost in our wanderings, but always can trust that God walks with us as we move ever toward the realization of God's vision.

Now it is time to sing, envision, enact, and retell a story of God coming unexpectedly in the worst of times as a baby born poor, born homeless, born to die that all human life might be transformed and dreams made real. It's God's good news—but only because we already know the story of Easter.

Christmas is a mystery, to be sure. There are four versions of God's good news. Mark's version, the oldest, is the one most interested in history, yet interestingly it has no birth narrative. We'll never really know how it all occurred; indeed, if we did, we might miss the truth of the story. John provides no account of the birth either, but that is not strange, for John's first concern is never historical fact. John is concerned about sacrament, that is, how God provides us with outward and visible signs of inward and spiritual truth. So John speaks of the Word becoming flesh and dwelling among us as light that shines in darkness (John 1:1-14). It is the two catechetical or teaching gospels, Matthew for Jewish Christians and Luke for Gentile Christians, that provide us with a birth narrative. Their intention is instruction. If we are to be informed, we will need to enter into the story as they tell it. And the issue for these storytellers is, "To whom did God come?" God entered human history for all people, but God came to a particular people, perhaps because only they would recognize God's coming. ·

God came and comes to those who are denied God's shalom but have waited in hope, those for whom the dream has become dim but who still long for its coming. And who recognized God's coming? The shepherds: those who were so busy caring for their dumb, dependent animals that they could not get to the temple to perform religious rituals. Why was it not the priests or people busy with ritual celebration? Could it be that our religious ceremonies become idolatrous, ends rather than means? Could it be that our busyness in the church prevents us from seeing the mystery of God's coming? It is worth pondering. Perhaps Christmas as we celebrate it can cause us to miss Christ's coming again.

Christmas—the mystery of possibility, the mystery of the saving power of God in our lives and history—is the mystery of a child. It will always be a mystery, for the world seems no better since that birth; some would argue it is worse, for we have assumed the power of God, the power to destroy all human life through the use of nuclear power. If we are looking for evidence of new possibilities, we had better not watch the evening news. If we are looking for evidence of progress in human history, we· had better not read the Sunday *New York Times.*

We Christians are a strange lot. When we are most faithful, we are like those unsophisticated, devoted shepherds: While going about their daily rounds longing for a new possibility, waiting in hope for a new possibility, living prepared for a new possibility, open to the mystery of God, they saw what only the eyes of faith can see. It is good news, of course, but it is also awesome, because it is only a possibility, the mystery of a baby in our midst. But that is enough, and so we come and bow down before his light and give thanks for the gift of sight.

As John would explain it, Christmas is a candle in the dark. Jesus was born in dark days; we live in dark days also. But somehow in that darkness a little light has been kindled, and nothing has been able to extinguish it. Indeed, its flickering light makes it possible for us to see the outline of new life amidst the darkness of our own lives, to see the outline of a new tomorrow amidst the darkness of the world's evil. And that flickering light, if we concentrate on it, provides us with all that is necessary for walking into the night. John's point is clear: We need to focus on the good. The problem of evil that most of us worry about may be the wrong problem. The really difficult problem is not why there is any evil, but why there is any good in the world. That small flicker of good is the Christmas mystery, the mystery of possibility that might grasp us if we don't surrender to secular celebrations of Christmas and escapist rituals that can creep into even the holy dark of midnight Eucharist or the holy light of Eucharist at dawn.

A few years ago a friend told me of standing before a painting in a European museum, Pieter Brueghel's "The Numbering at Bethlehem." When my friend first looked at the picture, he was puzzled. He could not see anything explicitly religious about it. The painting depicts a typical midwinter scene in a Flemish town of the painter's time. In the little snow-covered town the streets are filled with holiday activities. A wreath hangs over the door in one of the shops where a merchant and a buyer haggle over prices. A young man flirts with a maiden who is out on an errand. In the foreground a farmer and his wife butcher a pig for someone's Christmas feast. A laborer struggles with an overloaded cart of firewood. In the background children cavort and skate on an ice-covered pond or beg their mothers for a taste of pie. A crowd of people press in before the local tax office to be counted for the census and to pay their taxes. It is a typical busy, everyday, midwinter day, and life in the little village is going on as usual. Indeed there is nothing unusual in the scene, certainly nothing of any religious consequence. It is all secular, humdrum, ordinary.

But if you look more closely, you will see, down toward the bottom of the canvas, there in the middle of the street, unnoticed by passersby, a humble, stooped-shouldered man carrying a bag of tools and leading a small donkey trudging through the snow. And on the donkey, shivering from the cold, an old blanket thrown over her shoulders, is an unassuming young woman. It is Joseph the carpenter and his young wife, Mary, come from Nazareth to pay taxes. Emmanuel.

Is not this the way that the Christ comes to us, not just on Christmas Day, but every day? Moving in silently, without fanfare or burst of trumpet, coming into the midst of life in all of its everydayness and clutter and workaday concerns, arriving, as Paul said, "like a thief in the night" (1 Thess. 5:2). Here is God, touching and loving earth in the form of a baby, born to lowly parents in a stable. It is so easy to miss it.

We need the eyes of expectancy and faith. As John the Baptizer exclaimed, "There now stands among you, often unknown to you, the one who is your salvation" (John 1:6-18, 19-28). The impossible possibility, God is always entering our lives and our world to deliver and to save us. The problem is in our perceiving; our faith is fragile. It needs to be refreshed; and so it is, through the mystery of Christmas.

Christmas is past. The memory of Jesus' birth has been celebrated. We move on in time, wishing we knew more about the childhood and adolescence of Jesus. All we know is that his parents were Mary, a peasant girl, and Joseph, a carpenter who died while he was young. They were Jews, untouched by Greek culture, who spoke Aramaic and were active in the temple cult at Jerusalem.

Jesus began his ministry at thirty; it lasted a year or eighteen months. Almost all we know about him is restricted to that year. He was considered a controversial character, a teacher of liberal persuasion and most likely sympathetic to the liberal Pharisaic party. He was considered by many to be an interpreter of Scripture who spoke with special authority, and by others a prophet of God's reign. What little the historian can say about Jesus simply isn't very interesting.

The early church was not interested in Jesus' biography. But it did remember a few tales of his childhood and wanted them to be remembered. The modern church in its wisdom has assigned one of these stories to the first Sunday after Christmas (Luke 2:41-52).

For the evangelist Luke, this lesson serves as a bridge between Jesus' birth and his ministry. At Jesus' birth Luke the evangelist has God's angels announce his status and role as savior; during his presentation at the temple Luke has Simeon and Anna recognize him as the Lord's Christ; and at his baptism Luke has a voice from heaven address him as God's beloved Son. But in this story Luke allows Jesus to speak for himself and establish both his own identity and his understanding of faithful life.

The story is simple, but its meaning is not so obvious. Stories are remembered and told in special ways for special reasons, and in this case its importance is more than a passing interest in Jesus' childhood or family relations.

Jesus and his family had visited the temple on Passover. Assuming that Jesus was with other relatives, his parents left without him. Three days passed before they missed him; they returned and found him in the temple, where the altar of sacrifice was maintained. The parallel to Holy Week—to Good Friday, Passover, Jesus' sacrificial death, and three days among the dead—is intended. Not understanding, his parents rebuked him. Jesus responded, "Why were you looking for me? Did you not know that I must be busy with my father's affairs?"

Thus Luke has Jesus declare his identity as God's son and establish his freedom from everything that might deter him from living out that sonship. He truly accepted the call to discern and do God's will, over the claims of both self-interest and obedience to his family, just as later he would do the same in accepting the cross and denying the claims of both political and religious authority.

The message is intended to be clear: We are to do likewise. Jesus affirmed a new righteousness that was a renunciation of both self-serving and self-sacrifice. He objected to blind faith and blind obedience. He rejected any obligation to authority that leads to tyranny and any advocacy of individual freedom that leads to anarchy.

Bertolt Brecht's *Calendar Tales* (New York: Grove Press, 1966), is the story of a woman who for 70 years lived a life of devotion to duty. She raised her children, looked after the house, cared for her husband, helped him with the business, and gave up every personal pleasure. When she was 70 her husband died, the children left home, and she sold the business and started life again. This time she lived for herself: She refused room in her big house to needy relatives; she treated herself to numerous pleasures. She wouldn't visit her husband's grave or even associate with her children. For 70 years she had lived for her family. Her life was characterized by self-sacrifice; she was a selfless person responding to all their needs and reacting to all their requests. In the last years of her life, she did just the opposite. She sought only to meet her own needs and interests. She became a self-serving individual who lived for herself alone. Thus Brecht establishes two impossible ways of life, pushing the reader to imagine an alternative.

Some Christians believe that self-fulfillment, self-centeredness, and freedom are goals to be strived for. Recently social scientists have noted that a significant portion of our population are engaged in an egotistical search for their true selves. Rooted in American individualism is the conviction that the needs of the self rightfully take priority over the desires and needs of others. We live in a country built on the thesis of unlimited individualism, Darwinistic competition, and the conviction that society functions best when there is little government intervention and when each member is responsible for his or her own interests.

Some in the church learn to be selfless and some learn to be self-centered. The story of the young Jesus in the temple, told on this Sunday of the Christmas season, confronts both convictions and offers an alternative. Luke makes clear, from the very beginning, that no action of Jesus can be understood except in terms of his clear sense of positive identity. To know himself as God's child prevented him from living a selfish, or selfless, life. His sacrifice and obedience to God's will were acts of self-realization resulting from a sense of self-awareness. His death was the final substantiation of his identity. The more fully we are aware of our identity as children of God, the easier it is to let go of ourselves without denying ourselves.

Christ calls us to a life of thanksgiving for the reality of our salvation. We need no longer live for ourselves, nor do we need to deny ourselves. We celebrate the fact that we are loved and lovable. With thankful hearts we can respond by freely giving our lives in the service of our brothers and sisters. We no longer need live *selfishly* for ourselves, but for Christ! We no longer need live *selflessly* for others. We can love and serve each other for Christ's sake. As a grateful response to God's love, we can seek justice and peace. Thus Christ in and through us continues his response to God and his work of salvation for humankind.

One more story remains in Christmastide, those two weeks of celebrating the mystery of possibilities before Epiphany arrives (Matthew 2:13-15, 19-23). It's the story of a dream in which Joseph was warned that the birth of a possibility was threatened with extinction. That threat is ever before us. Even if we pray for possibilities, we don't always like their coming, for possibilities necessitate change and change is threatening. It is easier to live the known and predictable, even if it's not so good. That's why Herod was threatened. He benefited from the way things were. There is a little bit of Herod in each of us. Possibilities have implications. Births mean growing up. The baby may not be aware of it, but those of us who have grown old and are called to be reborn know that childhood isn't all a lark. Most of us—no matter how joyful or sorrowful life's experience has been—do not want to go through childhood again. We would prefer to skip it, if not to eliminate it all together. But struggle with rebirth we must, for the eternal cycle goes on and the birth of possibility at Christmastide will become the naiveté of childhood in Epiphany.

Seven

Living Naively

On Christmas we celebrate God's coming to us. On Epiphany we celebrate our going to God (Matthew 2:1-12). One of the names given this "supreme day," as the Middle Ages referred to it, is the Feast of the Three Kings. Of course they were not kings; nor were they men for sure, nor were there three for certain. Though tradition has given them the names Melchior, Casper, and Balthazar, we do not know whether they were black or white, nor even from the east. From the critical perspective of the historian, there were no such three kings. The three kings live only in the eyes of our imaginations, and their poetic story is only for those who believe in the truth of dreams and the longings of the human heart. Epiphany is the festival of dreamers. People who hear voices, see visions, follow stars. Epiphany is the festival of childhood and the eternal characteristics of children whose intuitive way of knowing outstrips their intellectual development and earns them the label "naive."

Recall the words of the little boy Amahl in Gian-Carlo Menotti's opera *Amahl and the Night Visitors*: "Oh Mother, come and see, there's never been such a sky. Damp clouds have shined it and soft clouds have swept it as if to make ready for a King's ball. . . . Hanging over our roof is a star as large as a window and the star has a tail and it moves across the sky like a chariot on fire."

Wearily his mother replies, "O Amahl, when will you stop telling lies? All day long you wander about in a dream. Here we are with nothing to eat, not a stick of wood for the fire, and all you do is worry your mother with fairy tales" (© 1952, G. Schirmer, Inc.).

Who but imaginative, naive, childlike persons and mad magicians envision—let alone go in search of—a child who on love alone will build a kingdom, whose pierced hand will hold no scepter, whose hallowed head will wear no crown, whose might will be built on people's toil, who will bring us new life and receive our death, whose kingdom belongs to those in need? Just such a visionary quest is the mystery of this childhood festival of Epiphany.

On Epiphany we celebrate the story of that blessed journey taken by all those who seek after God's reign. The story we tell is a story of our human journey illumined by the poetry of three wise pilgrims, led by, of all things, a star, through deserts and hazardous unmapped wilds, just to catch a glimpse of a longed-for ruler of earth and heaven. It is God's story, but it touches our human story in a way that only Easter equals; this explains why Epiphany was the second greatest festival in the history of the church year. We are all pilgrims in search of fulfillment and health, holiness and wholeness, peace and justice, equity and freedom. These foolish wise folk, these naive, childlike characters were looking for God's kingdom, for the way to individual and corporate salvation in the world and in their hearts. And they found it by obeying the foolish wisdom of their imaginations; by acting as if their dreams were reality; by paying no attention to the way things really are, and risking a journey in search of an impossible dream. They let intuition take precedence over intellect, imagination over reason. It was a long, mad, lonely journey into a land some call fantasy land. They were classified as naive and dismissed by learned and practical folk.

It will always be so when we follow the longings of our hearts. Those who act upon dreams and follow stars are rare in an enlightened age. We prefer to live with certainty. We have difficulty accepting chaos and surprise. We find it difficult to give our lives to anything we cannot be sure of. When we are engrossed in necessary, practical, everyday affairs, it seems ridiculous to place our confidence in the unexplainable, to surrender our lives to what we cannot see, and to live for the impossible. It appears so foolish, impractical, naive, and irresponsible. Witness the reaction to those who would make peace through unilateral disarmament. Only a naive child would think of such a crazy idea. Epiphany is an invitation to go on a journey we cannot order or control, following a way we cannot fully comprehend. Like Frodo, J. R. R. Tolkien's strange hero, we will have to endure the terror of encountering monsters and dragons. Yet like Frodo, if we go on this terrifying adventure, we need to go with both faith in miracles and the conviction that everything will turn out for the best.

People who hear heavenly voices and see visions and follow stars are not the folk we typically admire or want our children to model. Not long ago there was a newspaper account of a wealthy retired corporation executive who in his retirement worked eight hours a day, against his family's best judgment, as the sexton in a Roman Catholic church. One day he was dusting a statue of a saint and he heard a voice say, "Go sell everything you have and follow me." The voice was so real that he went to the bank, withdrew all his funds, wrote a single check, left it in the church's poor box, and headed out of town to find a monastery. When he didn't return home, his family reported his disappearance to the police, who soon found him. When his family heard what he had done, they put him in a private mental hospital for observation. Soon he was dismissed as "mentally unstable" but harmless.

Once there was a man named Anthony who heard the same voice and went to live in the desert. Another man, Francis, heard the same voice while kneeling before a statue of Anthony. Both Francis and Anthony the church named saints; this modern man was almost labeled mad. The feast of Epiphany invites us to listen to the voice of God and step forth on a spiritual pilgrimage; to enter a new secular year forgetting all that lies behind and ignoring all that seems reasonable today; to trust in the possibility of God's dream and go forth carrying with us the gold of love, the incense of longing, and the myrrh of suffering. Epiphany invites us to live as the mad *Man of La Mancha* who dreamed the impossible dream and strove with the last ounce of courage, to reach the unreachable star.

On the first Sunday after Epiphany, God's story turns to Jesus' baptism (Mark 1:7-11), Jesus' call to ministry that is our call to ministry. Along with the Easter vigil, this is the most important day on which to celebrate baptisms in the church, for it reminds us of our necessary human response to God's gracious act. God makes us a new people and our world a new world. We are called to respond by living in the world in ways that reveal to others that the possibilities of God are realities. We are to live so that when people look at us, they will see a manifestation of the life they long for and dream about, and when they see us acting in this world, they will see a people who are naive enough to believe that God's reign has indeed begun. There is no time in the year when the implications of our baptismal covenant become more clear. Listen to what we promise:

> To continue in the apostles' teaching and fellowship, in the breaking of the bread, and in the prayers;
> To persevere in resisting evil, and, whenever we fall into sin, to repent and return to the Lord;
> To proclaim by word and example the Good News of God in Christ;
> To seek and serve Christ in all persons, loving our neighbors as ourselves;
> And to strive for justice and peace among all people, respecting the dignity of every human being.
> (*The Book of Common Prayer,* pp. 304-05)

Now is the time to ask how well are we doing, and to commit ourselves once again to ministry.

As the story continues through this wonderful season of childhood—naiveté understood not as a chronological age or developmental stage but as a characteristic of all human life—we are reminded over and over again of what it means to take the Easter story seriously in our day-to-day lives, what it means to be a visionary people who will risk living for dreams. The story then turns to Jesus and his followers (John 1:29-41). John had his followers also. One day Jesus passed by and John said to his followers, "Look, over there! the Lamb of God." And Andrew ran over and asked Jesus if he could join him. Jesus welcomed him and Andrew ran off to fetch his brother Peter, saying, "Come and see." And that is what God's story is about. Come and see, or perhaps better, show and tell. Evangelization involves inviting people to live with us in the church so that they can experience and see a manifestation of the Gospel and hear the story that explains why we live in such a strange manner. Of course we need to have something to show them, and we need to know the story. But at the very least, we need to remember that we are to be sacraments of Christ, outward and visible manifestations of God's spiritual truth. And on this week we are reminded of that truth. "Come and see!": That is what God's story is about and what our story needs to be about.

The story now changes to the arrest of John and Jesus' going forth to proclaim by word and example the good news of God's reign (Matthew 4:12-23). "Acts-evangelism" we might call it. We easily forget that the book is entitled "The Acts of the Apostles" and not "The Talk of the Apostles." Too many people think that we will convert the world through sermons alone. Not so. It is through our actions that we will convert people; our sermons will help them understand the reason, the motivation for our actions. The Word of God (upper case W) means the activity of God, not the words (lower case w) of the Bible. Social action and evangelism are not two different ministries of the church. Epiphany makes that clear. There is one ministry: It unites God's story and our human story in a way of life that offers others an experience of the truth we have experienced.

A story I once heard goes like this. The family of the three little pigs had settled down comfortably in their brick house in the suburbs. Years had passed since the crisis with the wolf. Gradually boredom set in. One day the three pigs decided that what they were missing had to do with love, and they determined to go out and seek love's meaning. The first little pig went to the university library and read all she could on the subject of love; when she had finished she had learned a great deal about love, but her life was still empty. The second little pig read in the newspaper that a famous pig was coming to town to deliver a series of sermons on the subject of love. The second little pig attended all the sermons and was filled with enthusiasm and emotions. His emotional high lasted four days, and then his life became pretty much as empty as it had been before. The third little pig invited two other pig families over to their house one evening and all three little pigs began to share their life stories, continuing till late in the night. They found this so interesting that they decided to meet together regularly to share experiences and life together; in time they came to care about each other very deeply. One evening, after the other families had left, the third little pig said to her siblings, "Now I know what love is, for I have experienced it."

To be a true evangelist is to offer to the world an experience of the good news. And when they ask you why you act in such a way, then you can tell a story about Jesus, a story that explains why you do such naive, "silly things." Epiphany calls us to acts-evangelism.

In another Epiphany story Jesus opens his ministry by spreading the word that God's long-awaited, long-hoped-for rule has begun (Mark 1:21-28). Of course, it wasn't any more obvious then than it is now. Therefore, what everyone needed to do was repent, that is, change the way they perceived reality and behave accordingly. "You see," said Jesus, "only the eyes of faith can make the invisible visible. And only those who risk living as if faith were true will ever know if it is." And soon after he began, he set out to find students.

In those days teachers convinced students to come live with them. (I'm just as happy we don't do that anymore, though I am sure it is the best way to teach.) Jesus convinced a few fishermen to be his students, and on their first Sabbath together he took them to the local synagogue for a lesson. As always, a small group of others gathered about to listen. What Jesus had to say, as you might guess, was startling. But what everyone present noticed was that here was a teacher who didn't just talk; he acted as if he really believed what he said. First, Jesus taught that God was saving the world from all that distorts human life. Then Jesus drove out the evil in the demon-possessed person. Now that was really strange, for then as now, most of us who teach advise our students to do as we say but not as we do. So most of the students were really impressed, though they still wondered about his teachings. New ideas are never easy to grasp, let alone believe. "Here is really a new teaching," they exclaimed, "but what is really astonishing is that this teacher provides evidence to support his teachings. Here is a teacher who deserves to be taken seriously." And students hearing about this unique teacher flocked to hear him talk and observe his behavior. And the other teachers in their jealousy sought to defame him and point out the evils in his teachings. Some things never change.

The story of this Sunday in Epiphany challenges us as the church to teach as Jesus taught, by putting word and deed together: for unless we do so, our teaching will have no authority. If we want our children to have faith and the world to believe, we will need to talk less and to act more. Now if you are anything like me, you wish that were not true. But it is. If we are to teach as Jesus taught, we will need to make sure that the Gospel we preach is the Gospel we live. For only if our words and actions are consistent will our teaching command attention. The good news of God's reign, which is the content of the Easter story, cannot be grasped without difficulty. Insofar as seeing is believing, and given the fact that we do not see, it is a difficult message to believe. Only if we in the church believe enough to act as if it were true will others catch a glimpse of God's gift of a new humanity, a new world, a new social order.

I recall the early days of my ministry. It was in the days of large youth groups. I had about three hundred young people in a large room one night, while two more were in the kitchen making popcorn. I well remember, because the two got very loud, "I'm going to put salt in the popcorn." "You're not going to put salt in the popcorn." "I'm going to put salt in the popcorn." Then a body came crashing through the wooden door—he'd put salt in the popcorn!

Well, in the chaos these two characters copped out and I was left with a mob of screaming youngsters. "What are we going to do with them?" they asked. "They've done nothing but ruin everything since kindergarten. . . ." Having no idea what to do, I said, "Well, why don't we just sit down and talk about it?" At midnight there were still about twenty students left. They decided they were going to pay for the door out of their own pocket and invite the two back next week to make popcorn—as one said, "In two bowls."

I turned to a sixteen-year-old girl and I said, "Tell me, why'd you just do such a silly thing?" And she replied, "Isn't that the way God treats us? We keep messing up, but God does more than just pay for a door. God suffers for us, to show us we are loved anyway. Tonight I was just trying to show I was a little grateful."

During the early civil rights movement, I was working part-time for a religious news service. It was a time when everybody was looking for a "good news" story. Readers always complained we didn't publish any, so I went trudging off to find a good news story. And I found an integrated church in the deep South. I remember going to a leader of the congregation and saying to him, "Explain to me why you did this." And he answered, "Well, we didn't do it because it was more just. We didn't do it because we believed in human dignity. We decided to do it because one day we had to face up to the issue of how we could be the church if everybody couldn't eat at the same table."

The story for the fifth week in Epiphany reminds us that we are the salt of the earth, the light of the world (Matthew 5:13-20). We are to provide an example so that others might see what is hidden by darkness; we are to bring out and preserve the essence of what is present in the world but not obvious. Be an Epiphany of the Easter story for others, says the story, but remember that your intentions must be as holy as your actions. If we give money to the beggar to get rid of the beggar or to be admired for caring for beggars, we haven't been a true Epiphany. We are to love our enemies and those who persecute us—love not in the emotional sense of "like" or the intellectual sense of "think well of" but in the active sense of "seeking the good of" others even when they intend evil for us. Love has one aim: to bring about God's shalom, God's reign of justice and peace, freedom and equality, unity and well-being for all.

There is an old tale told by the rabbis that if a carriage turns over on both an enemy and a friend, one is to care for the enemy first. For by caring for the enemy first you have not only performed an act of love, but you have made a new friend and love has served its greatest purpose—to remove hatred or, perhaps better, to bring about reconciliation. The case is clear that we are to be *doers* of the Word. Still, most of us would rather study the Bible than act upon it.

Then comes the last Sunday of Epiphany, and the story turns to the Transfiguration (Matthew 17:1-9). On this Sunday before Ash Wednesday and the beginning of Lent, we pray, "Strengthen us for what is to come," and we tell the story of Jesus with Peter, James, and John on a mountaintop having a mountaintop experience.

We are not told Peter's frame of mind at the beginning of the story, but we can presume it was not particularly joyful. While he may have been pleased to have been chosen as one of the three to accompany Jesus to the top of the mountain to pray, it was only about a week after Jesus had first told them that he would suffer, be put to death, and rise again. Recall that Peter had tried to change Jesus' mind, and that Jesus had rebuked him, saying, "Get behind me, Satan. For you are not on the side of God, but of humans." We can presume that Peter's spirits were low; and whether from that weariness of spirit or the fatigue of the climb, the story explains that Peter and the others fell asleep.

When they awoke they were amazed to see a vision of Jesus talking with Moses and Elijah. Peter was so enraptured that he did not want this heavenly vision to end; and when it seemed about to, as Moses and Elijah were leaving, he proposed staying there awhile and offered to build three booths to accommodate them. His offer was not only ignored, but interrupted. A cloud overshadowed them, and God made the point that Peter had missed. "This is my Son, my Chosen, listen to him!" Not possess him or use him to sustain your happiness but *listen* to him, particularly when he tells you that glory comes only through suffering. Peter and the others had to go back down the mountain with Jesus.

Many of us, like Peter, have had our transfiguration experiences. Perhaps we have never thought of them as such, but for most of us the experience of God has come bursting into our ordinary lives, if only fleetingly. Perhaps it was the experience of witnessing the miracle of birth, of gazing at the vast expanse of stars on a quiet night, or of seeing the beauty of creation transformed by another sunset. Or perhaps it was a powerful though not particularly pleasant experience such as seeing an old friend slowly but gracefully give up the gift of life. At times such as these we are stirred inside, for we are aware that we are in the presence of God.

And like Peter we say, "Lord, I don't want this to end. I want always to feel like this. Let me stay here."

But like Peter we cannot live our lives on the mountaintop; we must come down to the plain. We need to learn that we cannot possess these moments, these special occasions when we are aware of God's presence among us. We can only enjoy them for what they are and for as long as they last—and try to learn from them. We must learn to live naively, but that is not the whole story.

If our tendency at first is to hold onto those experiences, our temptation as time passes is to dismiss and forget them. Nevertheless, they are reminders of a loving, magnificent God—who is always present—whether we are consciously aware of it or not.

In other words, Jesus was as much the Son of God, filled with the radiant life of the Spirit, on the plain as he was on the mountain. Peter and the others were just grasped by that reality on the mountain. So too, our occasional glimpses of divine reality do not cease to be valid simply because they fade into our memories. Though they may later seem to have been an illusion, we must listen to our transfiguration experiences because they point us to the ever-present power of God. Our ordinary perception limits us to the surface of life, leads us to the illusion that there is nothing beyond it, and keeps us bogged down in our disappointments and confusion. Our extraordinary glimpses of the divine reveal to us the heighth and breadth and depth of the God who loves us and is with us always.

Like Peter we wonder in awe at those moments when God breaks through the sleep of our lives to show us his glory. But let us neither attempt to possess nor later dismiss such moments. Rather, let us give thanks for them and allow them to be what they are, times of deepening and strengthening.

And so the season of Epiphany is about to end; Lent is about to begin. The story of the transfiguration has provided us with a glimpse of God's presence in Jesus. It is also a reminder that heavenly glory does not eliminate suffering. Only those who have suffered the pains of existence are entitled to wear halos: no cross, no crown.

During Epiphany we have celebrated promise and possibility. We have moved from Christ's call to our call, from

God's mission through *him* to God's mission through *us*. And as the season closes, we are provided with a vision and a reminder that what we preach is not ourselves but Christ crucified. We are treated to a mountaintop experience and reminded that we cannot stay there. Or to put it another way, we are reminded that we cannot live in the real world of suffering and evil without mountaintop experiences and visions. So amidst a season of living in our imaginations, of living for a dream, we are again given a glimpse of the vision to sustain us, but reminded that we need to take seriously the negatives of life, the cross and its suffering. The life of Martin Luther King, Jr., is an example. One who dreams suffers, because suffering is inherent in any dreamer's life. And that brings us to the end of a season in which mission and ministry, evangelization and social action, are dominant in our lives, and in which another dimension of God's story and our story intersect.

Eight

Facing the Principalities and Powers

There comes a time in our human pilgrimage when we become aware of lost innocence. The naiveté of childhood comes to an end and we face up to the hard realities about ourselves, others, and the world. Epiphany closes and Lent, characterized as the season of adolescence, begins. Having attempted to live as childlike dreamers for eight weeks, we turn to reflect on how we have done. It is the adolescent struggle for identity and purpose all over again. Just as childhood is more a recurring characteristic of life than a chronological age or developmental stage, so adolescence repeats itself over and over again. As persons and as the church we examine our interior and exterior lives. Aware that God accepts us just as we are and offers us forgiveness for the times we have denied who we really are, we enter a penitential season in the church's eternal cycle. Penance: acts of making whole again and repairing damage done, and of growing in grace and living into who we really are.

Perhaps Lent can best be understood through the example of a spiritual exercise known as the examination of conscience. It begins by taking us back to a time in our lives when we experienced grace, wholeness, and health. It asks us to live once again in that grace. Having bathed in that holiness of life, it asks us to examine our lives and identify the brokenness and incompleteness we have experienced, the evil we have done, and to bring this experience to God in contrition. Then we are to imagine God transforming our brokenness into wholeness, our incompleteness into completeness, our evil into good. Once transformed, we are to ask God to reveal to us what new behavior will demonstrate to the world our healing. Once clear on how we ought to live, we imagine ourselves living in that way and experience God's presence with us. And last we celebrate the new grace in our lives.

Lent, like every other season, is lived in the light of Easter. But just as every Advent we open ourselves to being pregnant with God once again, and every Christmas we give birth to a new possibility, and every Epiphany we live in the naiveté of childhood dreams, every Lent we face up to the struggle to acknowledge who we really are and the continuing battle with the principalities and powers in our lives and history that prevent us—not entirely against our will—from actualizing our true identity. Lent is that serious, contemplative time when we prepare for the renewal of our baptismal covenant that we will make at Easter. Easter is the key to the church's story, but without a holy Lent, its power is diminished. The stories told during Lent help us to face up to our temptations and the ever present threat of evil; they help us to face up to the ways in which we need to die and the narrow gate through which we need to pass; they help us to face up to our blurred visions, misplaced loyalties, and wrongful desires; they help us face up to our blindness and to the healing and nourishment we need; and they help us to face up to the ways in which we are bound and trapped.

It all begins on Ash Wednesday. Jesus warns us in the gospel about showing off our religious practices in order to gain favor with God or other human beings (Matthew 6:1-6, 16-21). We gather to communicate with God and to begin the church's season of personal truth-telling, for that is what Lent is about. Those who receive the imposition of ashes on Ash Wednesday are saying something about themselves. We are fragile beings. Each of us knows people whose lives have been snatched from us. And our own life, no matter how stable, how secure, how satisfying it appears to be, is but a transient splash in the rapids of history. We flourish, and in a moment we are gone. That's not gloom, that's life. Still, it is important to remind ourselves of our mortality; the ashes of this day drive home that sober truth.

But if that were *all* the truth, this day might well become morbid. The truth of God that summons life from the ashes is a promise that the giver of life continues to give life even when we distort it. We live securely, not because of our own strength, which can pass quickly in the night, but because of the God in whom we live and move and have our being (Acts 17:28). It is by God's gracious gift that we have life. It is not our possession. It is a gift entrusted to us from God who loves us. Our bodies will go back to the earth whence they came. Our lives are not dependent on what we possess, not even on our bodies and their fragile strength. We are dependent, finally, on the God who keeps giving love and creating life. That is a sober truth, but a hopeful one that turns the seriousness of Lent into serenity. Dependent on God alone, we enter a time to explore what we are doing with God's gift of life, so in grateful love we might give back what is ours for a time and God's for eternity.

Lent invites us to risk a journey through death to life, to enter a wilderness filled with danger, to enter the desert where both God and the evil one dwell. It's a journey that has been documented in the *Legend of the Holy Grail,* Dante's *Divine Comedy,* and Tolkien's *Lord of the Rings.* Like Frodo, Tolkien's unprepossessing hero, we have to endure the terror of encountering monsters and dragons in the underworld if the new, the transforming, the miraculous, are to be breathed into our lives. All too often the church has offered us only feasts without fasts, talk instead of silence, togetherness instead of solitude, satisfying tasks instead of suffering, a vacation trip instead of a wilderness pilgrimage. But each year at Lent we are invited to enter the desert, to embrace solitude and silence, to fast, to open ourselves to suffering, to listen for the voice of God in our restless spirits.

No sooner had Jesus been baptized than he was driven into a wilderness (Mark 1:9-13). I doubt that is the way we would have written a story about God's entrance into history, but it surely made sense to the writer of that gospel. He knew that any moment of the day or night a knock might come at the door—a knock that for the baptized might mean being thrown to the lions for public entertainment or being turned into a living torch for one of Nero's gala parties. Is it any wonder then that Mark's account of the aftermath of Jesus' baptism has him taken into a dark dangerous wilderness with an invitation for us to follow him?

An old Hasidic tale may help us understand this truth. A poor Jew named Isaac lived in a hovel far from the city. One night Isaac dreamed that if he made a long difficult journey to a far-off place he would find a bag of gold under a bridge leading to the main gate. It seemed foolish, but he made his way painfully and slowly to that place. He arrived weary and hungry, tired and sore, and found the bridge heavily guarded. Forlorn, he told the guard of his dream, but the guard only laughed. "You old fool! Only last night I had a dream that if I were to journey to a small village, I would find a treasure behind the fireplace in the miserable home of an old Jew named Isaac. Be off, old man!" Isaac made his way home and so at last found the treasure.

The meaning is easy to see. The treasures we seek are close to us, but in order to discover them we must go on a long fearful pilgrimage that leads through the wilderness. Once again you and I are invited to go on that journey to find our lives.

Let me tell you about an experience I had recently. Tuesdays are long teaching days for me. I often do not have a chance to eat. On a certain Wednesday, after just such a Tuesday, I left to go on retreat. It was one of those travel days when meal times and flight times do not overlap. "I'll eat later," I thought, as my stomach growled once again. Then I felt my temper rise when I discovered that my bags were lost. The plane was late, and when I arrived at the retreat house, I was told there would be no time for a meal. We would need to leave immediately. It was getting dark, and I was going on a *poustinia*, the Russian word for desert. A *poustinia* is a retreat intended to reproduce the experience of Jesus' temptation in the desert. We hiked for two hours to a small cabin. Inside I found a wooden cross about my size, a wooden slatted bed without mattress or blankets, a worn Bible, a candle, and an icon of Mary the Mother of God. My guide left me a small loaf of bread and a bottle of water. She said that I would be picked up in three days and that she would pray that God's angels would care for me.

I was very hungry. Besides, when I get troubled—angry, hurt, anxious under pressure—I have an enormous desire to eat and my ambition to be a gourmet cook emerges once again. At that moment I could think of nothing except food. I went to bed hungry and dreamed I was at a huge dinner party with only bread and wine. In the morning I took a hike and in front of me I saw a tree covered with grapes. I returned to my hut and read the story of Jesus' temptation, and my torment began. What does food represent in my life? From what evil do I need to be delivered? From what do I need to be protected?

God's story and ours keep intersecting. Imagine Jesus on retreat, in order to discern God's will for his life. He fasts and meditates on Scripture. Hungry, he thinks of these words from the Deuteronomic scroll: "God subjected us to hunger and then gave us manna to eat, an unknown food, in order that we might learn that we do not live by bread alone but on whatever bodily nourishment God gives" (Deut. 8:3).

Surely Jesus was aware of the rabbis' commentary on these words; they had made it quite clear that Moses was not referring to the significance of the spiritual or the insignificance of the material. To the Hebrew mind the material and the spiritual can never be separated. Moses wanted people to remember that God could and would meet all their human needs, but that God would do so in God's way. God would sustain them physically and spiritually by the divine providence, sometimes with bread and sometimes with manna and sometimes with something else. God wanted them, as God wants us, to acknowledge, on the one hand, human needs and limitations and, on the other, God's unlimited power and desire to meet human needs. All life is dependent on God's word, or better, on God's will. As Jesus meditated on this word, he became conscious of how difficult it is to give up control and independence. Tempted as we are, he gave himself to God's will; so instead of living for bread, he became the bread by which the world can live.

Scientifically speaking, we humans may be classified as *homo sapiens,* thinking persons, but from a religious point of view, we are dining persons. All animals eat, but only humans dine—eat with ceremony. Feasting and fasting are at the heart of the Christian life. During Eastertide we feast, during Lent we fast. Before each weekly Eucharistic feast we are not to eat breakfast—not to break-the-fast—so that we can learn to feast on whatever God provides. "Happy are the hungry," says Jesus in his Sermon on the Mount. "Feed my sheep" were his last words to Peter. "Feed on Christ," counsel the same Medieval theologians who established gluttony as one of the seven deadly sins. "We humans do not live by bread alone," Jesus told his tempter. Yet he taught his students to beg, "Give us bread daily."

Too many folk give up superfluous food during Lent, and too few seek the food that God offers. Lent is the season to remember how easy it is for us to forget that we are dependent on God's grace for life. We act as if we have to do it all ourselves, and we seek to be independent and in control. Is it any wonder that we have difficulty witnessing to the truth of the master?

The story of the second week is the story of Nicodemus and being born again (John 3:1-17), of becoming childlike, that is, dependent, nonrational, and nonproductive, even though we have become adult. In our culture, being adult seems to mean being independent, rational, and productive. We like being in control, practical, and reasonable. Of course it is difficult to live the Easter story when we live that way; so, even in our old age, we need to be born again.

When we do, we will be enabled to recapture those characteristics of dependency, imagination, wonder, and prayer: that nonproductive life of contemplation, solitude, and silence, of giving up control and listening to God. This life of prayer and contemplation is not an escapist activity banished to the private sector of life, an activity having no effect on the social order. It is, rather, the foundation for rational, moral social action. The new birth Nicodemus is called to is a life of prayer directed toward the vision of God's reign. Prayer that lacks this futuristic orientation is bound to produce that false peace against which we are constantly warned. Christian prayer is inseparable from resistance and struggle. Complacency and the absence of inner torment are the deadly enemy of prayer. Searching in darkness, struggling for the narrow way, aching for fulfillment, embracing suffering are signs of new life, of living prayer, of unity with God.

False peace, in fact, is a kind of paralysis, an illness of the body, an adult disease. Deliverance from this paralysis is one of the signs of God's reign and new birth. False peace is an attempt to escape from reality, sometimes by intoxication with chemicals or mental illness. The coming of God's reign is associated with the casting out of demons. Nicodemus needed to be born again. So do we all, over and over again. The test of our spiritual life is whether or not we are living as a new people in a new world, living in a constant and actual friendship with God, aware that we are restored to God's image, infused with God's spirit, empowered as saints of God to live the new life of childhood wisdom and naiveté on behalf of God's new world of justice and peace. Of course that means we will need to die, but that is what Lent is all about.

And that brings us to the story for the third week of Lent (John 2:13-22). This story has been used to support so many different causes that it is hard to break open its meaning afresh. Certainly its meaning is not self-evident. Today's gospel narration is found in all four versions of God's good news, though John as always tells it somewhat differently. The basic story is simply this: Jesus came to Jerusalem, went to the temple and drove out all those who were either buying or selling within the temple gates. As he did so, he combined quotations from the prophets Isaiah (56:7) and Jeremiah (7:11) who in God's name had exclaimed, "My house shall be called a house of prayer for all people, but you have made it into a business enterprise, a tourist trap."

John is not interested in historical accuracy. Literalists will always misunderstand him. While Matthew, Mark, and Luke have this event occur at the end of Jesus' life, John places it at the beginning. John also makes a major point of establishing its occurrence at Passover—that high festival season celebrating the sacrifice of the Paschal lamb that marked the salvation, the liberation of the Israelites from bondage in Egypt. Only in John did the authorities ask Jesus by what authority he had acted. Jesus—as is typical in John—ignored their question and gave an answer to another question, which, as you might guess, confused them. He said, "Destroy this temple, this symbol of God's saving activity, this embodiment of sacrifice for your salvation, and in three days I will raise it up." Now it had taken forty-six years so far to build the temple, which was not yet finished. And so they didn't understand the "three days" until after his crucifixion, the sacrifice of his life, and his resurrection, when the disciples remembered his words. They find expression in our liturgy each week when we exclaim, "Christ our Passover is sacrificed for us; therefore let us keep the feast" (*Book of Common Prayer*, pp. 337, 364; cf. also 1 Cor. 5:7-8, *Book of Common Prayer*, pp. 46, 83).

In the middle of this symbolic narrative Jesus drove out with angry violence (only in John did he make a whip of cords) the merchants in the temple. Some have used this episode to justify Christian violence on behalf of some good cause. Conservatives have used it to justify the righteousness of war, with Jesus as the patriotic militarist; and liberals have used it to justify civil disobedience, with Jesus as the revolutionary. Both have misused the text. Angry violence is out of character for Jesus, but symbolic prophetic acts are not. So in this case, what is the point?

First, it was a religious obligation, and one Jesus accepted, that at least once in one's lifetime a faithful Jew should make a pilgrimage to the temple in Jerusalem and fulfill two other obligations of offerings or sacrifices to God in gratitude for all God had done for the people in saving them from bondage in Egypt and leading them through the desert to a good land. One offering was in the form of a tax—a half shekel is mentioned in the book of Leviticus—and the other was an animal offering mentioned in the book of Exodus. A group of entrepreneurs were simply earning what they considered a legitimate profit for providing a convenience, that is, enabling the pilgrims easily to fulfill their religious obligations. They were able to buy clean animals instead of having to carry them over the long journey from home, and the merchants exchanged the Roman coins most people used for legal tender with appropriate money for the temple offerings. I think immediately of foreign money exchanges at airports, for whose services you always pay a pretty penny. Now on the surface that seems innocent enough, but from Jesus' perspective something more significant was going on. And what was at stake has its contemporary parallel in the saying, "If you have it, flaunt it."

Jesus was upset about the root sin manifested in that temple business activity. A root sin is in fact not a sin but a disposition toward sin, a disorderly affection that estranges us from our true selves, from God, and from our neighbor. It is our human propensity to turn proper means into improper ends: to be idolatrous.

The Christian faith is materialistic, that is, it asserts the incarnate unity of the material and the spiritual. But this holy alliance can easily get out of balance, and the spiritual can be lost. There is nothing sinful about wealth or money or possessions of talents. They are all occasions for grace, and properly understood are means toward spiritual ends.

But they are always occasions for sin when they become ends in themselves; then what is good becomes sinful. That is what had occurred among the faithful in Jesus' day.

Perhaps also in our own. In his book *To Have or to Be?* (New York: Harper and Row, 1976), psychoanalyst Erich Fromm contends that two modes of existence are struggling for the spirit of humankind: the *having* mode, which concentrates on material possession, acquisitiveness, power, and aggression and is the basis for such universal spiritual evils as greed, envy, and violence; and the *being* mode, which is based on love, in the pleasure of sharing, in concern for the good of others, and in meaningful and productive rather than wasteful activities. The having mode has been dominating our lives and bringing us to the brink of psychological and social disaster. And that is what today's gospel is all about.

Our Western industrial society has become centered upon things rather than people; greed for money, fame, and power characterize our world. Even the English language has been changing from one dominated by verbs to one dominated by nouns. A noun is the proper denotation for a thing. We say we have things. How often do you hear people say I have a degree, a job, a friend, security, a problem or even "it." We possess and we are proud of it. And we consume, which is one extreme form of possessing.

Because our society is devoted to acquisition and consumption of things, we rarely see much evidence of the being mode. Avarice, the love of possessing, has become a national root sin, and our economy and well-being are founded on buying what we do not need. Our appeal is to "the man who has everything." Who of us has escaped? Rich and poor alike have made having more important than being, have turned the love of our possessions into the love of possessing, have turned proper material means into improper ends. Jesus' day and ours have much in common—and so back to our gospel.

Today, as throughout his ministry, Jesus is the one who

heals those who are sick, brings wholeness to those who are broken, cleanses those who are diseased, casts out those demons that destroy us, saves us from our distortions, rescues us from our sins. On this Sunday we are invited to reflect on the ways in which we live a distorted life, a life that denies the image of God within us and refuses to open ourselves to Christ's cleansings. On this Sunday we are encouraged to invite Christ into our lives so that he might drive out of us all that is not holy. We will then be able, in faith, recognizing his love, to come to his thanksgiving meal to be filled with his life.

The fourth week of Lent opens with a story that is simple enough—although its meaning is not (John 6:4-15). It is Passover time. For John almost everything really significant happens at Passover or is to be understood in the light of Passover. Noticing a crowd heading his way, Jesus, the teacher, decided to use the occasion to give his students a quiz. He said to Philip, the retiring, faithful, but perhaps least intellectually gifted of the twelve, "How are we going to buy bread for so many folk?"

Philip failed the quiz when he sadly responded, "We don't have enough money."

Andrew, the student always eager to please or come to another's aid, but typically not able to think clearly, blurted out, "There's a boy with five loaves and two fish," and then, realizing that five loaves is about enough food for one hungry teenager's lunch, admitted, "But that isn't enough!"

Jesus, aware that his students not only failed the quiz by providing the wrong answers but didn't even understand the subtlety of his question, made the decision to provide a learning experience rather than a lecture. He said to them, "See if you can get everyone to sit on the grass." Then he took the bread, offered thanks to God, and passed out the bread. After everyone was apparently full, Jesus asked his students to gather up the remains. And guess what! The bread that began as five small loaves filled twelve large baskets. As you probably remember, everyone was amazed or, should we say, wide-eyed.

That is why we still call this story a story of a miracle, or perhaps better, a sacrament—an outward and visible sign of an inward and spiritual grace. Once again John uses a story to communicate a sacred mystery. Its meaning is not obvious—even Jesus' students kept missing the point—and that is why literalists in every age will have difficulty understanding the church's story. In this case, John takes a beloved and remembered story and by retelling it in his own unique way shifts its emphasis so as to yield new meaning. John turns a story about a picnic into one about soul food. Dorothee Sölle, the German theologian, writes, "To live by bread alone is to die a slow and dreadful death. Of course, such a death by bread alone does not mean we cease to exist. Our bodies still function. We still go about the routines of life and even accomplish things. We breathe, produce, consume, excrete, yet we do not really live" (*Death By Bread Alone*, Philadelphia: Fortress Press, 1978, p. 5).

And thus we come to the last week in Lent and the story of the raising of Lazarus (John 11:18-44). It is a story that touches on the pathos of our human story. In one way or another we are all trapped—trapped by our lack of imagination, trapped by our experiences, trapped by conditioned responses, trapped by our social situation, trapped by limited abilities, trapped by seeming lack of power, trapped by our physical limitations, trapped by our family responsibilities, trapped by our addictions, trapped by our weakness of will—trapped and therefore without life. And the story is about how God can bring us back to life and make us witnesses to that new life. And that will be the story of Easter we need to hear again.

So we come to the end of Lent and prepare ourselves for the beginning of a new year, indeed for *the* beginning, for Easter is where it all began and where it always begins for each of us. The eternal cycle closes on a note of dying to our adolescent search for identity. It opens again on a note of rebirth to adulthood and the acknowledgment of who we really are and what we are called to live for, that others may know what is true for them also.

Nine

Seasons in a Community's Life

As we have journeyed together through the liturgical year, we have been experiencing the church as a story-formed community, a nurturing, caring, faith family, a liturgical people on a pilgrimage through seasons of profane time made holy by the eternal cycle of sacred time. We have also come to see that the purpose of a Christian faith community is to live God's recreative story so that it touches, illumines, and transforms our lives to serve God's purposes day by day as we live in relationship to God, self, neighbor, and the natural world. If these things are so, then perhaps we need to consider some radical reform of our church's organization, common life, worship, education, and outreach.

For example, most churches are goal-oriented, task-oriented institutions organized around a host of committees for education, social action, parish care, fellowship, education, worship, and the like. All too few of the church's members can retell God's story of salvation or share the ways in which God's story and their stories intersect. Most folk I know are unhappy about this situation and many are striving to correct it. What I would like to offer is a radical proposal.

I can imagine a parish with a vestry or some other official body to oversee the totality of parish life and to integrate its various activities along with eleven committees, one for each season in the church year: Advent, Christmastide, Epiphany, Lent, Holy Week-Eastertide, Ascension-Pentecost, three for ordinary time (one from Pentecost until the end of school, one for the summer, and one from the beginning of school until Advent), one for major festival days such as All

Saints' Day, and one for all lesser feasts and fasts. Each committee would consider worship, education, fellowship, parish care, service, social action, stewardship, evangelism, and the like within the context of its season. Each would plan, design, organize, and direct integrative activities appropriate to its season with a holistic view of mission and ministry in mind. Each season therefore would have a distinctive quality and yet be related to all the others. What follows are a few brief suggestions to stimulate imaginations and to give some concrete expression to this rather strange but, I hope, enticing idea for a nurturing, caring faith family engaged in service and action in the world. The suggestions are not intended to present a full-blown program inclusive of every necessary element. Their sole purpose is to be suggestive. Nevertheless, each demonstrates a way to integrate God's story and our stories in the church, as well as ways to witness to that integration in the world through living God's story day by day.

Holy Week-Eastertide: The story of a new beginning. The story of a royal passion, a cosmic drama, and the transformation of all life and history. Salvation: the victory of God, the triumph of good over evil and of life over death.

Passion Sunday: Salvation by grace through faith
Holy Tuesday: Grace as liberating love
Holy Wednesday: Grace as suffering love
Holy Thursday: Grace as reconciling love
Good Friday: Grace as redeeming love
Easter Vigil: Grace as transforming love
Second Sunday of Easter: Life in a sacramental
      community
Third Sunday of Easter: Life in a nurturing
      community
Fourth Sunday of Easter: Life in a caring
      community
Fifth Sunday of Easter: Life in a discerning
      community

Sixth Sunday of Easter: Life in a loving community

A season highlighted by liturgical celebrations and parish parties. The most joyful festive season of the year, celebrating the fact of Salvation, the birth of a new humanity, the establishment of God's reign in history, the Word (action) of God and life in the world to come. Throughout Holy Week every aspect of parish life and program might be focused on worship. Each day should provide a major celebration for children, youth, and adults. Passion Sunday could include the "Litany of the Palms" with an outdoor all-parish procession followed by a major dramatization of the whole passion narrative; Monday could highlight a community liturgy of reconciliation; Tuesday, a Jewish Seder; Wednesday, the celebration of Tenebrae and the end of Lent; Thursday, the beginning of the Easter cycle, Eucharist with foot-washing; Friday, the adoration of the cross; Saturday, a parish quiet day or retreat with final preparations for baptisms followed by the Great Vigil of Easter—the most glorious celebration of the whole year, highlighting the lighting of the Paschal candle, joyful processions with incense, baptisms, and a dramatic retelling of the salvation story, and standing "worthy before the Lord" at Communion. All penitential elements, including the confession, need to be eliminated and all redemptive elements including the gloria, alleluias, and festive decorations returned. This three-hour extravaganza for the whole congregation should be the most important celebration in the church's year; it is followed by Easter Sunday, the most festive celebration in the church year.

The five weeks of Eastertide are a time of parish parties and the suspension of all other activities except festive liturgies of a redeemed community. Liturgically, during this season a celebrative mood should dominate: the Paschal candle rather than a cross could lead the procession; confession could be eliminated, standing for Communion made normative; a major gospel procession with incense is proper, and a decorated baptismal font with water in it for blessings could dominate the nave. Just as education (cate-chesis) during Holy Week is consummated within the litur-gies, now it is accomplished through parish parties. *Week one:* A party for all those who are engaged in social action for justice and peace (sacrament in the world) and all those engaged in liturgical leadership (lay readers, acolytes, altar guild, etc.). *Week two:* A party for strangers, neighbors who are not in the parish, street people, the poor and needy and all newcomers. A thanksgiving dinner, perhaps with formal dress (provided free for the poor and needy). *Week three:* A party for all those engaged in shepherding ministries, such as church schoolteachers, parish care folk, and those involved in service in the community. *Week four:* A party for all those involved in the administration and organization of parish life. *Week five:* An all-church family party to celebrate common life together.

Ascension-Pentecost: The story of life in the Spirit. The story of the church being established as the body of Christ and empowered to be an Easter- and Spirit-filled people, to be the sacrament of Christ's passion, death, and resurrec-tion for all the world.

Ascension: Christ enters glory and commissions the
    Church (the community of faith) to be his
    presence in the world
Sunday After: Waiting for the Spirit as a powerless
    people
Pentecost: Empowered for mission and ministry
Trinity: Steadfast in faith and life as a life-giving,
    reconciling, perfecting community in the
    image of God.

A season to review seriously, evaluate critically, and plan intentionally for parish life; a season to celebrate the gifts of the Spirit and elicit commitment for the church's mission and ministry. A season to highlight stewardship.

A somber service on Ascension Day marks a church

returned to order, the beginning of serious reflection on congregational life. It is a time for every group in the church to examine critically its life and for the people to ask the extent to which their church is the sacrament of Christ, an outward manifestation of the Gospel in the world. In this way the whole congregation can prepare for the baptism at Pentecost. We baptize persons into a community of faith. We need to examine and reform our organizational and communal life at least once each year so that at the renewal of our baptismal covenant on Pentecost we can witness to a rebirth in church life. There isn't much time. The partying is over and we need to get serious and give extra attention to the reform of parish life. This is the time to do so.

Pentecost—assuming we have focused our attention on the necessary reform of our life—becomes a festive occasion to celebrate new life being infused into the church's life. The renewal of baptismal covenants and symbolic acts such as the extinguishing of the Paschal candle at the end of the last service or the praying of the Lord's Prayer (a symbol of the Christian life in community) in as many languages as there are nationalities represented in the congregation can make this birthday celebration also a commitment to living a new life in the Spirit. It is a time to celebrate the Spirit—the life— in the church and the variety of gifts and graces among us all—children, youth, and adults.

Trinity Sunday is an appropriate time to hold a weekend church fair. Booths can make everyone aware of all the various ways persons might involve themselves in the church's mission and ministry. Persons can sign up to participate, and workshops can be offered in which the knowledge and skills necessary for these various ministries can be learned. In this festive manner the church can prepare to enter ordinary time.

Ordinary Time: God's story continues in us as we live into our baptism. A season to learn to discern God's will for our lives and to be equipped for ministry through the acquisition of further knowledge and skills. A season to highlight the need to integrate our faith and our lives and to put our time and energy into Christian service and action.

A season comprising half the church year provides us with a time for sustained program and the involvement of the community in mission, ministry, and worship. Diversity, of course, is the key, but this season, even if it is broken up with summer holidays (which, by the way, give opportunity for events not possible during the rest of the year), will look like life in most congregations at their best. Church school classes might be formed to give children an opportunity to choose an adult to share experiences and reflections with them in various ways for a number of weeks. Or shops might be created in the church—for example, a study shop, lecture shop, reading shop, reflection shop, drama shop, music shop, art shop, project shop, audiovisual shop, experience shop, etc. Each of these shops might take the lessons for the day and help persons to look at their stories and the story through some particular activity in a shop as a way both to prepare for worship and to go forth "to love and serve the Lord." During the summer a one-week, everyday, all-day "camp" can be held to learn God's story through the arts as found in Hebrew Scriptures from Genesis through Deuteronomy.

Classes for adults and youth can be offered at various times to teach biblical interpretation and praying the Scriptures. Weekend retreats and "family camps" can be organized as means of integrating study, worship, and fellowship. Small groups of parents meeting in homes, business people in a restaurant, doctors in the dining room of the hospital, and so on can be organized to help people relate their faith to their daily lives and work. The illustrations are legion. Each needs to meet human needs in some particular social, cultural context. But for this period covering one-half the church year persons need to be encouraged to integrate their faith and their lives; to equip themselves for ministry; to grow in their understanding of the Scriptures; to be offered experiences of Christian faith and opportunities to reflect on these experiences; to study the social issues which face our world and to acquire knowledge and understanding to make complex moral decisions and influence public policy. It is not a time for the church to slow up its program, but rather to develop a sustained program aimed at equipping persons to live their faith day by day.

Advent: The story of recapturing a vision. The story of preparing for Christ's second coming. A time of four weeks to renew our relationship with God when we are weary in well-doing and discouraged by the darkness.

First Week: Watching in expectant anticipation
Second Week: Living prepared by changing the way
. we perceive life
Third Week: Waiting patiently in hope
Fourth Week: Giving up control and opening
ourselves to God

A season to emphasize solitude and silence, prayer and meditation. A season to highlight the spiritual life. A countercultural season. Four weeks to encourage the spiritual life, to slow down parish activity, to teach prayer, and to provide daycare so that everyone can attend morning and evening prayer each day of the week.

Liturgically this is not a penitential season, so the color blue is more appropriate than purple. We ought not to decorate until Christmas Eve. The Advent wreath with four white candles is enough until then. All unnecessary clutter should be eliminated from the church and a quiet, somber spirit maintained. The festival of St. Nicholas with an exchange of gifts (gifts that will contribute to a better world and be a sign of our Christian life, such as so many hours to care for the elderly as a gift of youths to their parents) is appropriate in this season. All catechesis might focus on the spiritual life, meditation, prayer, and contemplation. This

season can introduce all ages to the world of solitude and·
silence, enhance our imagination, and provide space and
time for activities of the spiritual life in this hectic secular
season of parties.

Christmas: The story of the birth of possibility. The story of
God with us now and always, supporting us in our anxiety.
Living for God's will alone. Life with God will not be a lark.
A season to discern where God is and where God is
calling us to be. A season highlighted by discernment. A
season dramatically different from Easter.

Candles and evening Eucharist, yes, but not candles for
all the worshipers and not a major festive occasion; rather a
quiet celebration. Decorating the church can highlight
Christmas Eve. Bringing in a crèche and the procession to
the crèche with the figures (minus the wise men of course)
can accompany the first carols. Perhaps some quiet times
together for simple parties to reflect on the significance of
incarnation and a sacramental view of life and to counter
our typical Christmas festivities.

Epiphany: The story of naive living. The story of dreamers
and visionaries. The story of our pilgrimage with God.
Childhood as a characteristic of life.

First Week: Life as covenant. Call to vocation.
Second Week: Life as revealing the light of Christ.
    Show and tell.
Third Week: Life as proclaiming the Gospel. Acts-
    evangelism.
Fourth Week: Life as word and deed. Teaching as
    Jesus taught.
Fifth Week: Life of living for the Gospel alone.
    Providing an example.
Sixth Week: Life as bearing a cross. Visionaries
    facing up to reality.

A season to get everyone involved in witness. A season to

highlight evangelism and social action. A season which can begin with a large children's festival or a parish party built on the imagination, such as an artists' dream party. A time for adults to recapture their childlike spirits. A time for the blessing of homes so that people can understand that the dream has to do with where they live. The Sunday following Epiphany, a major occasion for baptisms and baptismal renewal, to be followed by focusing all parish life and activity on evangelism and social action.

It is a season to get everyone—children, youth, adults—to engage in witness, so that living the faith rather than talking about it is dominant. All activities, parties, and the like need to be set aside so that action can dominate parish life. Learning by doing needs to be our focus. Coffee hours after worship should be spent in sharing what is going on outside the church and getting more people involved. It is a season for the discernment of God's will, moral decision making, and action. Education (catechesis) should focus on helping people to engage in mission and ministry, evangelism and social action.

Lent: The story of principalities and powers. The story of reconciliation and redemption. A time for sorrowful attention to our denials of who we really are as saints in the image of God, and of the world as the kingdom of God under the rule of justice and peace.

Ash Wednesday: Remembering our human
condition and God's unmerited acceptance of
us.
First Sunday of Lent: Wilderness temptations. The
need to be saved from trials.
Second Sunday of Lent: Estrangement from true
self. The need for new birth.
Third Sunday of Lent: Distortions and dissonance
in our lives. The need to be defended from
evil.
Fourth Sunday of Lent: Hungering for wrong

things. The need for soul food.

Fifth Sunday of Lent: Being trapped. The need to die to the world's understandings and ways.

A season to get our lives in order and to prepare the community for baptism. A time to grapple with the human problem. A season to highlight the transformation of our lives through God's grace.

The church's penitential season begins. A transition is needed. Shrove Tuesday provides a rite of reversal, a carnival day of feasting before the fast, a celebration to say farewell to alleluias. Then Ash Wednesday, a sobering somber day, and Lent begins. The liturgy needs to begin each week with the penitential rite. All flowers and decoration, including the reredos, if possible, should be removed. Candles should be limited to the altar. Purple is the color and bare wooden crosses should replace the gold cross in the procession and, if possible, elsewhere. Alleluias are out; silence after the lessons is in. The Way to the Cross can become a weekly devotion. Regular opportunities for the rite of reconciliation and the rite of anointing should be made possible. Kneeling for both prayers and communion should return. Simple meals and no refreshments at coffee hour. The congregation might consider a total shift in parish life, worship, and the church's environment. It is a time for serious reflection on our life experience, grace and sin, and a concentrated look at the story of salvation so that we might prepare for Easter baptisms and a new beginning. It is the reflective period in the church year, a time in which we strive to make sense of our experience and to understand the faith of the church.

There are, of course, other important holy days such as:

All Saints—(baptisms): Time to remember who we really are and the ministry of the laity, the people of God.

Ember Days: Time to reflect on the various ministries of bishops, priests, and deacons.

The Presentation: Time to remember families.
St. Mary: Time to remember mothers.
St. Joseph: Time to remember fathers.
Holy Innocents: Time to remember children.

And there are many lesser feasts and fasts.

While these comments are intended to be suggestive only, I hope I have demonstrated that God's story should dominate, direct, and control our life in the church and that our aim for this is authentic faith and life, faithful mission and ministry. Life in a community of faith—a nurturing, caring family, a story-formed community journeying through time—is essential to our life as an Easter people living into our baptism and pilgrimaging with each other and God, to the end that God's will is done and God's reign comes. To be such a community, our liturgical celebrations need to follow more closely God's story and the eternal cycle of the Church's year; our life together needs to be more supportive of human growth and development; our life in the world needs to be a more dramatic witness to the good news we claim; our catechetical life needs to bridge our ritual life and daily life as well as nurture our community life and prepare us for action in the world. None of this can be done adequately if we adopt a business-management, institutional model of the church; if we have weekly liturgies with no communal sense of participation by all ages in God's story dramatized over a sacred cycle; if we have education limited to a Sunday church school with its own curriculum and following a secular yearly cycle; if we have an organization that begins its fiscal year January 1, uses a program budget, and understands stewardship as church finance and evangelism as church growth. A new way to envision the church, worship, education, mission, ministry, stewardship, evangelism, and program are needed. I have suggested an alternative way to envision parish life; it is radical and risky but perhaps worth consideration.

* * *

So God's story is represented each year as an aid in our human pilgrimage, to intersect with our stories to the end that God's story is realized. God acts in human history through the passion, death, and resurrection of Jesus Christ, and all life and history are transformed. We live in the joy of that fact and celebrate its reality in our lives. We go forth to live accordingly, ever striving to discern better God's will and understand God's ways that we might love and serve God. But while these actions help us perceive life in new ways, the dream always seems to fade, the vision weakens, we get weary and become discouraged. And so we stop our busyness and turn once again to God. We wait in solitude and silence. Because we do, God comes to us again and reminds us of our calling. We give ourselves wholeheartedly to the manifestations of the vision we bear. But the principalities and powers in our world and our human weakness surface, and we need to admit the brokenness and incompleteness in our lives, turn to God in sorrow, receive God's unmerited transforming love, and learn what we must do to witness better to this grace in our lives, to the salvation we know. Having prepared our hearts and minds to live into our baptism, we come to celebrate once again the good news of the Easter miracle. So it is that we journey together in community to actualize God's good news about human life and history. A new reality has been established, and we are in the process of living into it. That is, with God's help we are actualizing what is already true, by ever acknowledging and proclaiming that God's reign has come, is coming, and is yet to come. Christ has come, Christ is coming, Christ will come again. We live between the here and the not yet, as bearers of a story about the good news of God.

A great deal, of course, gets in the way of living this story. We do not know the story well enough, we do not celebrate the story adequately; we do not strive hard enough to live the story faithfully. We let other stories, celebrations, and ways of life conflict with the story. Worse, we adopt other stories or let them be assimilated into our lives until it becomes difficult to know what the true story really is.

In the beginning of this book I established the importance of seeing life as a journey through time in a story-formed community. I have attempted to show how God's story and our human stories intersect, and how God's story gives meaning and purpose to our stories. The challenge, however, remains. How are we to transform our common life in the church so that we might be an Easter people on a pilgrimage with God to achieve God's purposes for human life and history? There are those who do not want to change life in the church because they know it will change their lives and they like life as it is. There are those who are reluctant to change because they are familiar with the way things are and worry that a change might disrupt the life they know. And there are those who desire and are willing to risk change as well as commit their lives to making necessary changes because they believe that the reform and renewal of parish life, worship, and action are important for their lives and for those of the next generation. For all these groups, I hope this book has been a challenge, a stimulus, and an inspiration. We need each other as we reflect on our common life and envision alternative ways to live together faithfully as a pilgrim people. May we have the courage and faith to struggle together to find a more faithful way to unite our stories and God's story.

So this chapter and this book come to a close. But this is also a beginning. My hope has been to inspire you to rethink your parish life and programs, to enhance and enliven your imaginations so that you might find ways to integrate your stories with God's story. The rest, of course, is up to you. God speed!